Resilience

bounce back from whatever
life throws at you

This edition first published in Great Britain in 2010 by
Crimson Publishing, a division of Crimson Business Ltd
Westminster House
Kew Road
Richmond
Surrey
TW9 2ND

A catalogue record for this book is available from the British Library.
ISBN 978 1 85458 544 8

Printed and bound by LegoPrint SpA, Trento

For Sarah and Flora, whose resilience is more than a match for ours.

'Our greatest glory is not in never falling, but in rising up every time we fall.'
Confucius

'Success is not final, failure is not fatal: it is the courage to continue that counts.'
Winston Churchill

Contents

Introduction   1

Part 1   Understanding resilience   7

Chapter 1 What is resilience?   9

Chapter 2 Where does resilience come from?   17

Part 2   Being resilient   33

Chapter 3 My resilient self – self-esteem and self-efficacy   35

Chapter 4 Can do, will do – optimism and opportunism   49

Chapter 5 Leave it to me – taking control   61

Chapter 6 No worries – dealing with stress and
               anxiety   75

Chapter 7 I'll be the judge of that – making decisions,
               cutting losses   91

Chapter 8 Getting better all the time – lifelong learning   109

Chapter 9 With a little help from my friends – making
               the most of other people   121

Chapter 10 I beg to differ – managing conflict   137

Part 3   Becoming more resilient   153

Chapter 11 Raising the bar   155

Conclusion   195

Appendix   197

Bibliography and further reading   203

Index   211

Acknowledgements

Many of the ideas in this book were developed in conversations with colleagues at Nicholson McBride, notably Sandra Aldridge, Alyse Ashton, Charles Barlow, Kate Brown, Des Christofi, Ruth Colling, Helen Fisher, Emily Frohlich, Nick Kambitsis, Rubina Patel, Emma Seward, Brian Stansbridge, Kath Timmins and Geraldine Ward. Jon Bennett, Jamie Hollyhomes and John Southwell of the talent management company ETS were our partners in developing the 'Nicholson McBride Resilience Questionnaire' (NMRQ), ably assisted by Kate Grayson's knowledge of SPSS. Thanks are also due to David Lester, Sally Rawlings and Lucy Smith at Crimson, and to Sharon Walker and Susannah Lear.

Our major debt, however, is to a group of 26 people who were kind enough to participate in a series of structured, in-depth interviews. Membership of this group – referred to throughout the book as the 'R-team' (or 'interviewees') – was as follows:

Haydn Abbott – Chief Executive, Angel Trains International

Alex Allan – Chairman, Joint Intelligence Committee; Permanent Secretary, Cabinet Office

David Andrews – Founder and Chief Executive, Xchanging plc; member of the Supervisory Board, Deutsche Börse

James Bardrick – Co-Head of Banking, Europe, Middle East and Africa, Citigroup

Virginia Beardshaw – Chief Executive, I CAN children's charity

Baroness Tessa Blackstone – Vice Chancellor, Greenwich University

Alan Buckle – Global Head of Advisory, KPMG

Ted Burke – Chief Executive, Freshfields Bruckhaus Deringer

Sir Andrew Cahn – Chief Executive, UK Trade & Investment

Richard Cuthbert – Chief Executive, Mouchel Group plc

Alistair Da Costa – Managing Director (Asia), DLA Piper

Amelia Fawcett – Chairman, Guardian Media Group and Pensions First Group LLP

Joe Giannamore – Founder and Managing Principal, AnaCap

Ivan Gunatilleke – Chief Financial Officer, Cable & Wireless, Worldwide

Dave Hartnett – Permanent Secretary for Tax and Commissioner, HM Revenue & Customs

Katherine Maddock-Lyon – Head of Customer Strategy & Transformation, London Borough of Barking and Dagenham

Peter Middleton – Chairman, Syscap Ltd

Donald Moore – Chairman, Morgan Stanley (Europe)

Charlie Parker – Chief Executive, Oldham Council

Anthony Salz – Vice Chairman, NM Rothschild; Chairman, the Eden Trust

John Smythe – Founder and Chairman, Engage for Change

Deirdre Trapp – Partner, Freshfields Bruckhaus Deringer

Professor Lorraine Tyler – Head of Centre for Speech and Language, Cambridge University

Steve Varley – Managing Partner, Markets, Ernst & Young

Sir David Walker – Senior Advisor, Morgan Stanley; Vice Chairman, Legal & General

Rob Whiteman – Chief Executive, London Borough of Barking and Dagenham

Members of the R-team provided many of the views and stories cited throughout the book, as well as some of the case studies. Quotes from them are (in most cases) presented in **bold**.

Introduction

This is a book about resilience — the ability to bounce back from tough times, or even to triumph in the face of adversity; to display tenacity, but not at the expense of reason.

From our earliest history, and across all cultures, the quality of resilience has been admired, even romanticized. While the heroes of fairy tale and literature have tended to be tall, dark and handsome, brave and true, they have also tended to be resilient, appearing at their best when most severely challenged. We are taught the story of the beleaguered Robert the Bruce, inspired by the efforts of a spider spinning its web — if at first you don't succeed, try, try again.

But resilience has other resonances. In physics, resilience describes the process by which objects revert to their original shape after being bent or stretched. In medicine, it refers to the ability of individual patients to recover from injury or illness. For patients, this resilience may reflect differences in basic anatomy or physique (some of us, it seems, have 'good bones' which make us naturally quick healers), but it also appears to reflect aspects of personality — strength of will, say, or optimism; the 'miracle recovery' made by the professional footballer or runner when faced with the prospect of missing a key sporting event, to take one well-known example.

With over 30 years' experience working with individuals and organizations in a variety of difficult situations, we have our own understanding and appreciation of resilience. Over time, we have come to recognize that some people are simply less fazed by setbacks than others, clearly showing more resilience, whatever life throws at them, than others. Such people are able to recast their objectives, even reinvent themselves, according to the demands of the environment.

In our experience, such people also tend to:

- Be open to new ideas (they are good listeners, keen learners and are prepared to try different approaches)
- Assume the best rather than the worst of other people
- Find opportunity and risk equally fascinating (recognizing that the link between the two is crucial to success)
- Embrace positive change
- See what needs to be done and be happy to lead the charge
- Prefer dealing in transparency and honesty rather than obscurity and deceit

We have also noticed that people who display these character-istics usually have two other things in common – they are en-ergized rather than overrun by crisis, and other people actively choose to collaborate with them.

As soon as we started to think seriously about the concept of resilience, we realized that it might be a defining characteristic of many of the individuals whose approach to people and problems we most admire. We were keen to find out more, and to pass on what we learnt to others.

We intend to do this not by providing exhaustive academic analysis but by drawing on the experiences of real-life people in a variety of situations, people we have accessed either through our work or a wider network of contacts. In so doing, we hope to find answers to four key questions:

1   What is resilience?
2   Where does resilience come from?
3   What is it that very resilient people do which distinguishes them from those less resilient?
4   What can we do to make ourselves more resilient?

In order to answer these questions, we first reviewed what is already known about resilience, then used this information (as well as themes identified from our own experience) to construct a new, 64-item personality test (the 'Nicholson McBride Resilience Questionnaire' – NMRQ), which was completed by a random sample of contacts. To make things clearer, on occasion some of these items have been slightly reworded in this text.

Alongside this psychometric work, we conducted a parallel programme of in-depth interviews with 26 individuals, whom we refer to throughout the book as the 'R-team' (or 'interviewees'). These people were chosen not only because they are required to display resilience on a regular (even daily) basis, but also because they have been exposed to – and bounced back from – exceptional challenges and setbacks. These challenges have been both personal and professional, including, in one extreme example, being caught up in a terrorist attack.

All the individuals selected have reached high positions in a number of different organizations — from banks to charities, industry to education — and are living proof of resilience in action! Although drawn from a work context, their experiences hold lessons for us all, whatever our age, experience and personal circumstances.

We believe that we have identified the key elements that contribute to resilience — ways of operating that help protect certain individuals from the difficulties that plague the rest of us ('charmed life syndrome') as well as patterns of behaviour which underpin an individual's ability to tolerate stress and display courage and ingenuity in the face of adversity.

Crucially, we believe that these skills, attitudes and behaviours can be refined, developed or, in some cases, learnt from scratch. Of course, while an individual's capacity for resilience may be affected by their genetic make-up, genes exert their influence by setting outer boundaries, beyond which further development is impossible. Given all the factors which prevent us from reaching our full potential, it is unlikely that these boundaries often present a real barrier to development. On a more proactive note, there is considerable evidence to suggest that well-judged interventions (whether this is a teacher early in life, or a trainer or mentor in adulthood) can have a significant and sustained impact on behaviour, and even underlying personality traits. We really can learn to become more resilient!

As we write this book, the world is still trying to recover from the 2008 'credit crunch', which sent shock waves through the global financial system and provoked varying degrees of economic gloom around the world; squeezing jobs, security and confidence in the process. But this is not a book specifically about surviving the effects of the credit crunch (or, indeed, any other downturn), though, of course, hard economic times undoubtedly make many people's lives significantly more challenging. The truth is, life can throw us a curve ball at any point in our lives, and it can come from any direction – home, work or the wider world. The big question is how you deal with it; do you try to block it, dodge it or go for the sweet spot and hit it out of the park? Do you try to absorb the shock of the situation, avoid it or turn it to your advantage?

This is a book about how to survive, even thrive, in tough times – whatever their cause. It is about bouncing back, stronger and better than before. It is about developing your natural powers of resilience, and applying them over a lifetime.

Divided into three parts, Part 1 of the book seeks answers to the questions 'What is resilience?' and 'Where does resilience come from?'

Part 2 then moves on to consider the skills, attitudes and behaviours you need to join the ranks of the resilient, as identified by our research.

Finally, Part 3 is all about how to do it – how to build your powers of resilience. Starting off with a short questionnaire to establish your personal Resilience Quotient (RQ) – and identify areas of relative strength and weakness – the rest of the learning is built around a practical, 10-point plan which pulls all the advice and insights together, helping you to raise, and then sustain, your resilience.

An Appendix details some extra findings from our research.

Part 1

Understanding resilience

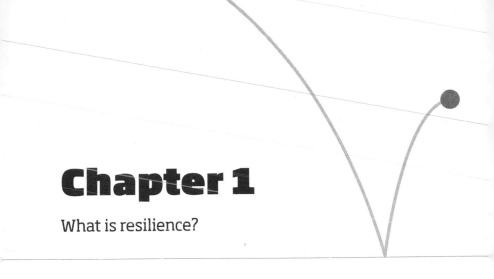

Chapter 1

What is resilience?

Resilience may be a universally admired and useful quality, but it has attracted surprisingly little attention from psychologists interested in individual difference — the study of why one person differs from another, and what makes each of us the person we are.

Historically, the concept of resilience seems to have been of interest more to doctors (struck by the observation that people who remain calm about serious illness tend to recover most quickly), to management consultants (especially those employed by organizations which need to offer a constant level of service to customers, 24/7) and to developmental psychologists (concerned with the effect of trauma on children).

Resilience has also been studied because of its close connection to change. Of course, any change causes a certain amount of turbulence — whether in an individual's practical circumstances or private emotions — and tests personal resilience. Change is a normal part of life.

However, while we have all got used to a certain amount of change (and the mantra 'change is the only constant' has descended into cliché), the expanded message of change is that we live in a complex, dynamic and connected world where the only safe bet is that what worked for us last year probably isn't serving us so well this year – and certainly won't do in the next. How fortunate, then, that as human beings we have more than 100,000 years' experience of evolving and adapting!

Having said that, we must be wary of falling into the comfortable assumption that, although change is a constant, it is changing at a constant rate; we merely need to make the same level of adjustment year on year to stay on terms. The fragility of such assumptions was exposed by the 2008 credit crunch, when a sustained period of easy money, spiralling house prices and economic growth came to a shuddering halt.

During the crunch, many of us came to realize that the financial system on which we had relied to protect our jobs, homes and pensions was, in many ways, a house of cards – sustained at the top by a combination of greed, chutzpah and the willing suspension of disbelief. Only the injection of huge sums of public money averted complete collapse. As a lesson in resilience, neither the system nor many individuals emerged with much honour.

WHAT'S THE SITUATION?

Of course, resilience can mean different things in different situations. For someone diagnosed with a terminal illness, resilience will be about trying to get the very best out of the time they have left to them. For someone in a war zone – witnessing death and destruction, and experiencing unimaginable emotional turmoil – resilience will be about keeping themselves and their family alive.

In genuinely traumatic situations, the American psychologist Dr Ben Weinstein suggests that the most common reaction among those directly affected is resilience, and that most people, with time, heal of their own accord. Weinstein was on the scene in the idyllic island of Phuket, Thailand, on 27 December 2004, just one day after the earthquake-induced Boxing Day tsunami hit. Sweeping across the Indian Ocean, this devastating tsunami wiped out more than 200,000 people, destroying the homes and livelihoods of millions of others in the process.

Faced with this unheralded catastrophe, Weinstein noted that many people demonstrated resilience by moving into survival mode, searching for food, water and other basic needs. To help with this process, Weinstein set up a buddying system, pairing up people of the same nationality so that they could help each other find shelter. As he remarked: '[These individuals'] communities, families and livelihoods have been shattered. In order to hope for good mental health outcomes, we need to help them rebuild their communities and social networks.'

Most people reading this book will not have had direct experience of disaster on this scale. Nonetheless, we are all still susceptible to stress and trauma in our lives. It might not involve surviving a tsunami, but all of us have to face challenges to our resilience, for example, the trauma caused by the death of a family member or friend. The bereaved frequently experience significant stress, depression and feelings of guilt. Similarly, illness — whether our own or that of someone close to us — tests our ability to bounce back and regain control.

Or the problem might be professional. Criticism, disappointment and disaster in the workplace can undermine our self-confidence and provoke a vast array of negative feelings.

For some of us, our sense of self-worth is inextricably bound up with our material status. We tend to judge how we (and, by comparison, others) are doing – our level of success – according to such indicators as the size of the house we live in, the car we drive and the money we earn. An amalgam of these indicators gives us our identity and sense of purpose, and determines how we think of ourselves – our self-esteem. A significant setback on any one of these fronts weakens our confidence about who we are and what value we're adding, whether to work, home or society.

While comparing ourselves to others is a natural response, it is not necessarily a healthy one. As Stephen Covey, bestselling author of *The 7 Habits of Highly Effective People*, put it: 'Did you ever see an unhappy horse? Did you ever see a bird that had the blues? One reason why birds and horses are not unhappy is because they are not trying to impress other birds and horses.' Related to this, our research makes it very clear that the most resilient people rarely experience envy. It's not that they're unemotional, rather that they're able to harness the galvanizing power of emotion while remaining immune from its more negative effects.

You may manage to avoid making comparisons between yourself and other people, but your identity and self-esteem will still be intimately informed by your relationship with others – for example, your role in the family. Again, a setback on this front can have serious implications, as noted by the psychologist Dr Gaithri Fernando. Like Ben Weinstein, Fernando was on the scene (this time in Sri Lanka) shortly after the tsunami landed. An expert in post-traumatic stress (particularly as a result of extreme trauma, such as war), Fernando found that, after two to three years, many of the Sri Lankans who had survived the tsunami had recovered, integrating the trauma into their new identities. However, she feared that this recovery might not be evident among those survivors who had lost close relatives: 'Who would they be fathers, mothers, sisters or brothers to now?'

As we have noted, some people are more resilient than others, but why? Why do some people seem better able to bounce back from whatever life throws at them than others? To understand this, it would be really helpful if we could identify our own individual resilience threshold, If there were some universal indicator which could show our personal 'tipping point'. But there's no easy way to do this; individuals respond differently to different events. What's more, one individual might be immensely resilient in one regard but not in another, and sometimes in quite surprising ways. Take the young man whose mother was killed in a car crash and whose father then committed suicide. With support, the young man handled this devastating series of events incredibly well. People were surprised, therefore, when he appeared to crumble on receipt of some relatively minor criticism at work. He could handle the bereavement but not the negative feedback; this was the final straw for him.

We are all unique in how we respond to situations and events. The trick, therefore, is to raise our own self-awareness. We need to understand what sorts of events are likely to affect us negatively, and then be alert to these happening. If a potentially harmful situation cannot be avoided, then it needs to be handled in as positive a way as possible. You have to bounce back as well and as quickly as you can.

OUR RESEARCH

This is the backdrop against which we began our investigation into resilience. We discovered a long list of qualities which earlier researchers had identified as key strands of resilience, for example:

- Facing down reality (being almost pessimistic in your view of a situation)
- Ritualized ingenuity (always finding solutions when faced with a challenge)
- Being able to exploit the positive events in life
- Proactive problem-solving
- A tendency to tackle issues rather than avoid them
- Early recognition of the need to change
- Critical understanding (keeping things in perspective and seeing beyond immediate chaos)
- An ability to search for meaning in life
- Knowing where to look for assistance

Since different researchers had conflicting views about the relative importance of these factors, we decided to create a new questionnaire – the Nicholson McBride Resilience Questionnaire (NMRQ). We constructed a questionnaire containing 64 questions, which tested those factors already established as being indicators of resilience as well as themes which had emerged from our own experience. Early results from the NMRQ indicate that the following 23 factors are strong predictors of an individual's overall Resilience Quotient (RQ):

- I am optimistic
- I have a positive mental attitude
- I can often create success from disaster
- I feel confident and secure in my position
- I wouldn't describe myself as an anxious person
- I am good at finding solutions to new problems
- In a difficult situation, my thoughts immediately turn to what can be done to put things right
- I rarely feel insecure
- I am good at anticipating problems
- I am calm in a crisis

- I've generally found that things turn out in an advantageous way for me
- I am good at seeing the silver lining
- I influence what I can rather than worry about what I can't
- I don't tend to avoid conflict
- I don't tend to take criticism personally
- I generally manage to keep things in perspective
- I try to control events rather than being a victim of my circumstances
- I manage my stress levels well
- I rarely worry what other people think of me
- I always try to take control of a situation
- I am generally good at proactively dealing with problems
- I trust my intuition
- I don't tend to get stressed easily

We then explored the interconnections between all 64 questions in the NMRQ to derive five key elements which we believe are central to resilience. In descending order of importance, these are:

1. Optimism
2. Freedom from stress and anxiety
3. Individual accountability
4. Openness and flexibility
5. Problem orientation

Each of these five elements is associated with a distinctive pattern of attitudes and behaviours; these are explored in Part 2. This, then, is the statistical answer to the question 'What is resilience?' But what does resilience mean in terms of real lives and experience? To understand this (and also the relative importance of these five key elements, and how they interact with each other), we conducted a parallel programme of in-depth interviews with the 26 members of the R-team. Their comments appear throughout the rest of the book (quotes are, in most cases, presented in bold). Here are some of their answers to the question 'What is resilience?'

> 'Resilience is the ability not to see failure as something to dwell on but as an opportunity to move forward, accepting that failure is a part of life.'

> 'Resilience is inextricably linked with responsibility. If you won't accept responsibility, you don't need resilience.'

> 'I associate resilience with not reacting too emotionally, not getting too fussed about what other people think. Resilience is about keeping your head.'

Chapter 2

Where does resilience come from?

So, we've described what resilience is, and why it is of value. Now we need to find out where it comes from and, more to the point, what determines our own individual RQ.

We know from our research that resilience isn't a simple, single dimension of personality, but that it has a number of distinct elements, at least some of which may be affected by genes. It would be astonishing, therefore, to discover that everyone's RQ is largely determined in the same way. However, when we asked members of the R-team 'Where do you think your resilience comes from?', we were surprised by how many common themes emerged.

There was broad agreement that RQ is not something that gets set once and for all, either at birth (by virtue of our genes) or even by the end of the childhood years, critical though these undoubtedly are. Significant events and influences throughout our teens and 20s – whether at school, university, travelling on a gap year or embarking on a career – can all have a powerful impact on personal resilience. As we grow older, life continues to be punctuated by challenges – opportunities for advancement as well as threats, even disasters – which not only test our resilience but can actually *increase* it. In fact, resilience appears to be an aspect of personality so powerfully influenced by experience that the jelly never quite sets; it's probably never too late to increase your RQ.

> 'I'm much more resilient than I used to be. In fact, there is a straight line graph through my career of growing resilience. In my work, you need to demonstrate resilience to secure promotion. It's one of the markers we use to select leaders.'

Having said this, every member of the R-team chose to return to the events of their childhood to explain how and why they have become so resilient. As one interviewee wryly remarked: 'You can pull people out of their comfort zones and challenge them, but real resilience tends to be born out of deep-seated experience.'

CHILDHOOD

From the stories the team told us, we identified five recurrent themes which help describe how childhood experiences inform resilience.

1 Troubled times

For more than half of the R-team, childhood was a troubled time. None of them claimed to have a vivid memory of their feelings as a child, but all agree that one result of their early experience was a steely determination, not just to survive that particular period but also, years later, to do whatever it took to ensure their own children didn't suffer in the same way. Some of them still sounded angry when they talked about their experiences, but they have all learnt to handle this negativity; indeed, many have turned it into positive energy.

'For me, resilience was built from surviving a difficult childhood. Of course, everyone hits tough times, but I learnt early that everyone also has a choice - you can either say to yourself, "Oh alright then" and give in, or "Right, let's deal with it" and search for other, even tougher, challenges.'

....

'My father was a labourer who, after 50 years' hard slog, had accumulated the scantest of savings. This made me very angry: the world seemed a hostile, unfair place. It made me determined to prove that I was as good as everyone else. Later, as I gained in confidence, this feeling was taken over by personal ambition - I thought to myself, "Let's see how good I really am".'

Unfortunately, not all children emerge unscathed from difficult childhoods — let alone manage to turn adversity to advantage. While our research does not definitively explain what it is that allows some people (and not others) to do so, it does highlight a number of key skills, attributes and behaviours which together promote reslience. More of this in Part 2.

2 Fish out of water

A second recurring theme among members of the R-team was an early sense of being different from others around them, a precocious understanding of the diversity of human beings, and the resulting need to develop different strategies for different people. Developmentalists call this 'psychological thinking', and it usually isn't much in evidence before the age of 11 or 12. Events forced some of our interviewees to display aspects of psychological thinking as early as five years of age.

'I went to a school where it was dangerous to be clever, but I learnt how to be successful without getting bullied. The secret was to be funny and also a bit rebellious. No one ever caught me working because I did it at home. I was always frightened, though, that people might find out where I lived and come and see me hard at work!'

....

'I was born in Asia to a privileged family, but was always aware of the terrible poverty many of the people around us endured; I remember registering this at the age of five. Following political upheaval at home, we had to come to the UK. Our wealth, however, did not transfer. It was a massive shock. I hated the schools I was sent to. I was a complete outsider a) because I was foreign, and b) because we had no money. I wasn't bullied as such, but I was isolated.'

Getting back on my feet

'I came from a large Irish immigrant family (my mother was one of 13 children), and although both my parents worked, the other kids at the school I attended were generally better off than we were. They tended to look down on us. The school was a convent, which valued compliance and conformity; I kept a pretty low profile for much of the time.

This all changed at the age of 15, when we took a family holiday to America - a country where introversion is not encouraged! Here I learnt to see myself in a different way, to push boundaries and not be afraid to express myself. I started to test my academic limits at school. Incredibly, my teachers were cross when I was offered a place at Oxford. This didn't really happen at my school, and they feared that I was getting ahead of myself.

Shortly after getting the good news about Oxford, however, I had a really bad car accident, which meant I spent the entire summer in traction; I also picked up a phobia about driving. I arrived at university on crutches, but this didn't get me down - being on crutches meant that I was distinctive and attracted attention. It also meant that I was more or less tied to my desk; I worked hard and ended up winning a prestigious prize.'

3 Unhappy families

The great Russian writer Leo Tolstoy got it right more than 100 years ago, when he noted in his novel *Anna Karenina*: 'Happy families are all alike, every unhappy family is unhappy in its own way.' This remains true today; indeed, the impact of family dynamics on individual development remains one of the most vexed topics in psychology. It raises many of the questions discussed on the psychoanalyst's couch and the problem pages of popular magazines.

None of the R-team was subject to the kind of physical or sexual abuse which makes the headlines tragically too often. A significant proportion of them, however, came from broken homes, or found themselves forced to act as stand-in carers. Several had parents who suffered from a range of disorders. As a result, the individuals concerned had to assume responsibility at an early age.

'My father was killed before I was born, and my mother led a very difficult life as a result; we moved around a lot. She could have caved in to circumstance but didn't, holding things together long enough for me to get away. Still, the financial and emotional strain did have a major effect on me; I quickly became aware of how fragile life is and the importance of having a roof over your head.'

'My childhood has affected me greatly. My mother brought me up to be confident; to always have a go and to be accountable for my actions. Her influence still looms large in my consciousness. My dad was not around so much. An engineer by profession, he was often away for long periods of time, which had a negative impact on my parents' relationship. Although I was one of four children, I was the only one to realize that my parents' marriage was in trouble. As my dad was away so much, I acted as a surrogate father to my younger siblings. I suspect I was more pompous, bossy and arrogant than

I should have been in my teens. In fact, my teenage years weren't a happy time for me. They were just about surviving. I was the boring one. Never took drugs, was always the designated driver - serious and responsible.'

'I had an unusual childhood. My mother was mentally ill throughout my youth. My father was very supportive, and put his career on hold. I also had a very strong grandmother, with whom I spent the first five years of my life. After my younger brother was born, my mother was hospitalized for six months. She underwent a lot of ECT treatment - so much so that she can't remember much about my childhood years. She also became addicted to prescription drugs. I felt responsible for her and my younger siblings from the age of nine. I guess I grew up pretty quickly.'

While many of the R-team had, in some respects, lost childhoods, they didn't let this deter them. Having responsibility early made them realize how much they were capable of, a realization they carried forward with them into adult life.

4 Strong role models

Of course, parents have a disproportionate influence on their children's development since they not only represent genetic continuity but also continuity of responsibility, in a way that teachers, sports coaches and others cannot. Responses to this parental influence can take many forms, ranging from imitation (role-modelling) through to rebellion, where the child rejects the values of the parent, at least in the short term.

'I was really lucky with my parents as role models. My dad could sort anything out without flapping. He was the sort of man who saved lives; for example, swimming across a river when there was a fire to rescue people.

One day someone lost their hand at the factory. Dad just picked it up, and took it and the guy calmly to hospital.'

'My father was quite a frightening man, but he had huge integrity. Whereas my mother was manipulative and dependent, he was open and independent. He set ferociously high standards. If I came second in the class, he would say, "Why weren't you first?" Still, I remember always feeling that my younger sister was his favourite. This spurred me on to achieve, to assert my individuality.'

'My parents weren't very touchy-feely, nor were my successes ever celebrated. I try to be different with my own kids. My elder brother was much cleverer than I was, but I was better at sport. After my father's death, I discovered that he had been hugely proud of my success – but I never knew it because he never showed it.'

Most resilient children benefit from active support networks. They tend to have a strong relationship with at least one adult, on whom they can depend, and from whom they can learn. This adult doesn't have to be a parent – and frequently isn't.

In her classic book *Love Despite Hate*, Sarah Moskovitz studied a group of children who, having survived Nazi concentration camps, were sent to a therapeutic nursery school in England. Those children subsequently judged to be the most resilient all considered one nursery-school teacher to have been the most potent influence in their lives. She had provided warmth and care, and had taught them how to behave compassionately.

5 A competitive edge

Sport is something most of us encounter early in life, whether it's through school, clubs or just messing around with friends. Not all children enjoy playing team games, but most need to let off steam, and this activity tends to develop a competitive edge; the playground and sports field is where many of us first test our limits.

Most members of the R-team share a love of competitive sport. Intriguingly, while few denied that they were interested in winning, they were at least as interested in their own reaction to defeat. For the R-team, defeat involves other key aspects of resilience – the ability to cut your losses and learn from mistakes, for example.

Members of the R-team use regular physical exercise (including participation in competitive sport) to maintain their fitness and guard against the effects of stress – both of which make a significant contribution to an individual's RQ. They also recognize the value of sport in preparing you for life's ups and downs.

> 'Sport is a great leveller; you can't always win so you have to learn to come back stronger than before. I am convinced that you can increase your resilience from a growing understanding that defeat is not the end of the world; that time will heal.'

> 'Athletics was incredibly important for me. It's the perfect place to experience the bitterness of defeat without it being life-threatening, and also to taste the sweetness of victory.'

Members of the R-team were convinced that their exceptional resilience as adults had its roots much earlier in life. Between them, the five themes or patterns described above encompass the childhood experiences of everyone we interviewed. However, most of our interviewees also pointed to critical challenges which came later – both in their professional and personal lives – which further strengthened their ability to bounce back.

YOUNG ADULTHOOD

Of course, your development doesn't stop when the school gates close behind you for the last time – far from it. Whether you're in your first job, away travelling or in further education, there's a good chance that your day-to-day interaction with friends, family and other significant people will change dramatically. Social networking sites and other forms of technology may help you to stay in touch with these people, but you're now spending your time with strangers, deciding which of them is worth investing in.

You also have to make decisions about how to organize your life – where to live, what job or course to take, whether to rent or take out a mortgage, and so on. You could be unemployed. One way or another, you are probably spending more time in your own company, and much of that time might be devoted to unfamiliar (and unwelcome) soul-searching. You may be asking yourself all sorts of questions: 'What sort of person am I?' 'Is this really what I want to be doing?' 'Have I made a big mistake?' 'Am I as good as I thought I was?'

The post-school transition period can be extremely challenging, resilience levels can be severely tested, and sometimes found wanting. It can also be a time when resilience grows dramatically; your belief that you can cope with most things may be reinforced.

> 'After finishing college, I went travelling with a friend. After a time, our plans diverged and I found myself taking long train journeys across India, alone - just me and a book in a compartment surrounded by people who didn't speak English. This was not how I thought things would be, but, ultimately, it turned out to be a valuable time for me; I sorted out a lot of things about myself.'

'I had a difficult time during my gap year in Africa. I found myself in situations that I just couldn't handle, for example, entering a village that had been completely deserted and having rabid dogs surround my car. For the first time in my life, I experienced real physical fear. I actually came home early, with the distinct feeling I had failed. My experiences affected my confidence at college. I also developed claustrophobia. Although traumatized, I remember thinking, "I'm not going to let this ruin my life". I dealt with my claustrophobia by deliberately pushing my boundaries, taking the lead role in a play, for example. Stuff happens, you've just got to get on with it.'

'I became pregnant at 20, got married and lived with my in-laws. We had very little money and I needed to start thinking about getting some work. I had my second child just as I was starting my first "proper job". Only two weeks after giving birth, I turned up to my first meeting. I thought to myself, "If I don't turn up, they won't ever give jobs to people in my position".'

'You can't do that...'

Sometimes, someone telling you can't do something is good for you - building mental toughness and conviction. L, who works in advertising, explains:

'Anyone with young children will tell you, if you ask them not to do something, they're guaranteed to do it. This is a something my dad used to his (and ultimately my) advantage.

As a child I wasn't particularly academic or ambitious, and certainly didn't work very hard at my studies. I never understood the importance of exams and, as a result, only did enough to get by. It wasn't until I was coming to the end of my fifth year - and facing the prospect of leaving school without any sense of what I wanted to do as a career - that I decided to apply to the local college to pursue further study. This, I thought, would buy me some time to explore my options.

Feeling pleased with myself for having made this monumental decision, I proudly announced my plan to my parents. My dad's immediate reaction was to say, "You'll never do that, they'll never accept you. You'd be better off applying for a job on the production line of the engineering works down the road. That's where your future lies."

I was so annoyed and upset by his response that I worked tirelessly for the remainder of the school year. In those critical few months I worked so hard I ended up winning three awards at the end of year prize-giving. The best part was being able to tell my dad that I'd been awarded a place at college. On hearing this news, he simply lowered his newspaper and, with a wry smile, said, "Well done, I always knew you would." He then carried on reading his paper as though nothing had happened.

This was my first experience of "reverse psychology". Some people might say it's a risky strategy, but it has certainly worked for me. It has been extremely valuable in both my adult and professional life, giving me the confidence, determination and motivation to succeed, even when the odds are stacked against me. Now, when a client rejects my ideas, I am not disheartened; I keep working, refusing to take no for an answer until I've exhausted all reasonable options.'

THE MIDDLE YEARS

Entering your middle years brings its own challenges and tests your resilience in new ways. Some people respond to this negatively (experiencing a mid-life crisis), while others recognize and build upon what they have achieved so far.

We believe that the development of resilience in mid-life is usually inspired by one of three factors:

1   The passing of time
2   Surmounting obstacles
3   Proactive boosting

1 The passing of time

Many people in their 20s are anxious about having to make seemingly irrevocable decisions – about work, home, choice of life partner, starting a family etc. It can all seem a bit of a roller-coaster, setting the course for their whole life.

A decade later, in their 30s, they may have learnt that some of these choices were actually far from irreversible, and their resilience is now being tested by having to cut losses, admit mistakes, change direction, let people down and burn bridges. There may be professional disappointments to be borne – you don't get the job or the promotion you want, you're made redundant etc. The 30s are really a 'make or break' decade, with growing responsibilities – at home as well as at work – and competitors to be dealt with in a way which ensures that you are where you need to be, personally and professionally.

However, it is the 40s that many people find the most trying. During this time, you might find yourself responsible for three generations – yourself, your teenage children and your ageing parents – as well as perhaps teams at work. If so, there's certainly no shortage of opportunity for your resilience to grow! By this point, you have acquired a portfolio of life skills; you may have mastered the arts of balancing and juggling, become more tolerant of ambiguity, and come to accept that circles have to be squared. You have had a chance to learn from other people's mistakes as well as your own. You might well have become more philosophical – realizing that mistakes and problems rarely constitute the end of the world – and more adept at handling those pesky curve balls.

2 Surmounting obstacles

The disasters of adulthood, like the challenges of childhood, can steer resilience levels in one of two opposing directions.

A serious setback can either knock your confidence – making you anxious that, when that type of problem happens again, you won't be able to cope with it; or it can strengthen your resolve, allowing you to learn from mistakes so you are better equipped to handle similar problems in the future. Resilient people recognize that failure and disappointment are often stepping stones to success.

Without exception, members of the R-team have encountered extremely difficult situations and problems, yet have managed to keep things in perspective, and bounce back stronger than before.

In the firing line

'I'm good at using my past experience to stop me panicking, and to help keep things in perspective. This came to the fore in November 2008 when I became caught up in the terrorist attack in Mumbai. I was in the restaurant at the Taj Mahal hotel when the shooting started, and was part of a group of people who barricaded themselves in down in the cellar. Essentially trapped, we spent a long time trying to decide whether we should do something different, or were better off staying where we were. In the end, we got out through the back of the hotel and found a hiding place.

There was a group of five of us, all quite high-powered – a chief executive, a couple of lawyers, an operations engineer and myself, a banker. Hierarchy and profession were soon forgotten, however; personality and skills were what counted. The engineer was brilliant at keeping up our morale, but most of the decisions were made by myself and the chief exec. The lawyers were hampered by their training. Lawyers are trained to analyze situations, but without data, precedent or any kind of formal framework, they became very anxious. They were certainly the least tactical and least well equipped to cope with what was a very frightening eight hours. It was very helpful to be used to thinking creatively, and in a fairly broad way.

We ended up in a wheelie rubbish bin, with bullets pinging all around us. I knew people were being killed, but funnily enough I never thought that I would be one of them. In fact, I've been more afraid as skipper of a boat I thought was going to break up in a tropical storm.'

'In my early 40s, I went to my doctor because of a suspicious lump. He told me it probably wasn't cancerous, but, unfortunately, he turned out to be wrong; I had to go into treatment. When I saw the surgeon he told me I had a choice - I could either sink into depression at the uncertainty of the situation or really immerse myself in my work, which was my passion. I did the latter, and my health problem did indeed go out of my mind. It was years before I could talk about what had happened, but the experience certainly made me a stronger person.'

'I had a really challenging experience in my late 30s, when my reputation could have been ruined. I was angry because clients had lied to me, although I did feel supported by colleagues. The whole thing lasted 18 months; it was exhausting. Still, I developed a powerful sense that I wouldn't let these people drag me down.'

3 Proactive boosting

So, your resilience will be affected – either positively or negatively – by how you respond to difficult life events. Of course, you may decide to take the bull by the horns and actively intervene in boosting your own resilience. You could, for example, engage the services of a coach, counsellor or psychotherapist; you could join a support group, seek spiritual sustenance or sign up for a programme of self-development – whatever works for you.

There is little doubt that personal resilience can be enhanced throughout life. But how do you do it? The next part of this book — Part 2 — is devoted to breaking resilience down into its key components and describing how these contribute to this vital resource. Part 3 then describes practical ways in which anyone who wants to can increase their RQ.

Part ②
Being resilient

Chapter 3

My resilient self - self-esteem and self-efficacy

When we asked members of the R-team 'What is resilience?' and 'Where does resilience come from?', their responses focused on the ability to achieve success, coupled with a strong sense of personal value or contribution. One interviewee put it this way: 'Resilience is based on two things – a belief in what you're doing, and confidence that you can make things better, even if only by 5%.' Another outlined four components of resilience:

1   Being comfortable with who you are
2   Being values-driven; feeling that you have to make a difference
3   Having other interests – a hinterland which provides a source of relief, even escape, and perspective
4   Having drive and determination (even ruthlessness) matched with realism – you can't win them all, so the knack is to pick the right things to lose on and then give in gracefully

Our research supports these views. The NMRQ clearly demonstrates that items relating to a positive attitude, the ability to make a difference and to take control of events, are highly correlated with confidence in your powers of resilience. We start this section, therefore, with an exploration of the effect that self-esteem and self-efficacy have on resilience.

WHAT DO THESE TERMS MEAN?

'Self-esteem' has been defined in many ways since first being coined by the English poet John Milton back in the 17th century, but here we link it to an individual's feeling of self-worth. Self-efficacy, on the other hand, relates to an individual's belief in their ability to achieve their aims. 'What am I worth?' is clearly a different question from 'How likely is it that I will succeed?' However, the terms are sometimes used as if they were interchangeable.

To be truly resilient, you need to give a positive answer to both questions.

Self-esteem and self-efficacy model

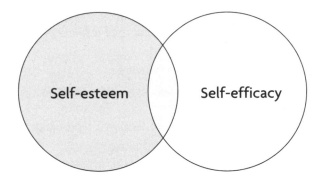

In the above diagram, the overlap represents pure, unswerving self-belief – not necessarily that the individual can achieve anything, but that they can achieve anything that is a reasonable stretch for them if they really put their mind to it. In the words of one interviewee: 'It's toughness and calmness, triggered by inner confidence. You know you're capable of doing whatever it is you are there to do.'

SELF-ESTEEM

In order to demonstrate resilience, you need a reasonably high level of self-esteem. You have to feel a sense of self-worth and self-regard in order to have belief in your own abilities (self-efficacy). Without this, you will struggle to find the necessary confidence and drive to bounce back from challenging situations. However, it is not enough to have occasional access to high self-esteem; you need to have it permanently 'on tap' if it is to constitute a stable resource.

Some psychologists say that high, but fragile, levels of self-esteem lead to narcissism – excessive self love based on self-image or ego. This is unlikely to result in resilience; indeed, it is likely to result in the opposite. Our interviews with the R-team revealed a degree of modesty, which contributed to their resilience. For example, when asked the question 'Do you consider yourself to be a resilient person?', many replied that they didn't see themselves as such, but that other people told them they were, so they must be! If high, but fragile, self-esteem results in narcissism, and low, but stable, self-esteem in humility, our R-team interviewees clearly occupy the middle ground.

Self-esteem also implies a degree of contentment, a capacity for happiness – not necessarily with the world, but with yourself. This helps you not to take things personally, and enables you to forgive others more readily. Self-esteem also appears to involve a protective sense of perspective, which counteracts the tendency for paranoid thinking to develop ('Why is it only me that this happens to?') and encourages the process of bouncing back ('What am I going to do to fix this?').

Some people appear to be blessed with higher self-esteem than others. This may stem from a loving and supportive upbringing – parents or other carers who reinforce a positive view of self. In our sample, however, the majority of the R-team attributed their resilience to a very different sort of childhood, one in which they were required to overcome challenge and difficulty at a precociously early age (see Chapter 2). Fortunately, we can all grow our self-esteem. This may happen naturally over time, or it may need to be more actively built.

In 2001, Jennifer Crocker, Professor of Psychology at the University of Michigan, identified seven 'domains' from which people most frequently derive their self-esteem:

1   Virtue
2   God's love
3   Support of family
4   Academic competence
5   Physical attractiveness
6   Gaining others' approval
7   Outdoing others in competition

In this list, the concept of 'success' is limited to 'academic competence' and 'outdoing others in competition'. Our research clearly indicates that a positive track record of results – whether at work, in the community or in some completely different sphere of activity – can contribute to a growing sense of self-esteem. We therefore suggest an eighth domain to add to the list – being successful.

No matter how high (or low) your self-esteem is currently, it helps to be able to identify its sources – what makes you think positively about yourself – as well as understanding clearly what can undermine your self-esteem – what makes you think negatively about yourself.

When you glance through Jennifer Crocker's list, do you alight on a clear winner? Does your competitive nature mean that, as long as you're doing better than everyone else, your feelings of self-worth are high? Alternatively, are you more buoyed up by academic competence – provided you're getting straight 'A' grades you can feel good about yourself? If you find that you have just one main source of self-esteem, you might need to be a bit careful; if academic competence is where you derive your feelings of self-worth, what happens when you fail an exam? Or if you think highly of yourself because of your physical attractiveness, how will you cope with ageing, or a disfiguring accident?

Those with a high RQ talk about the need to be rounded, to have a variety of interests and drivers in their lives. This makes good sense – if you have a number of sources of self-esteem, you will more easily be able to take setbacks in one area, and be more resilient as a result.

> 'Resilience involves self-confidence, sometimes almost to the point of narcissism. Compare Bill Clinton's response to being impeached with that of Richard Nixon. Nixon's reaction was entirely defensive, wanting to close everything down and suppress information. Clinton was totally confident in the support of the American people - that they would judge him on his wider record - and was prepared to gamble that they would back him, whatever was revealed about his personal life.'

> 'Resilience might sometimes look like arrogance - not listening, being thick-skinned.'

Interestingly, while self-esteem can help you to be more resilient, it doesn't necessarily make you more successful. Several pieces of research have indicated that students perform less well in experiments where attempts were made at enhancing their self-esteem. Psychologists argue that boosting self-esteem can lead to complacency; students try less hard and subsequently fare worse at exam time. So, while self-esteem may be derived from success, it doesn't necessarily create it.

SELF-EFFICACY

As discussed in Chapter 2, many of our interviewees suffered troubled, if not traumatic, childhoods. They encountered difficulties and setbacks which frequently made them determined never to allow the same to happen again, and to protect their families from suffering in the same way. This determination bred success, and high levels of self-efficacy. Indeed, most of our interviewees were confident that they could handle pretty much anything that came their way. And this belief was borne out of positive experience. Self-efficacy breeds self-efficacy.

So, why is self-efficacy important when it comes to resilience? Well, first and foremost, in order to demonstrate resilience, you need a challenging situation to deal with. People with high self-efficacy are more likely to be excited by challenges and view difficult tasks or situations as diversions rather than roadblocks; they are not knocked off course easily. Undaunted by the unknown, they take a broad view of the task in hand in order to establish the best way forward. And they demonstrate significant tenacity in dealing with problems. People with lower self-efficacy, on the other hand, assume that tasks are harder than they are; they worry about encountering failure rather than focusing on achieving success. They may prepare thoroughly, but since they tend to take a narrow (and sometimes short-sighted) view of a challenge, their planning is not always focused on the right priorities. When life throws you a curve ball, self-efficacy is one of the most important personal resources to have at your disposal.

Mind over matter

Self-belief can take you a long way, as the following story illustrates:

'I was involved in a London-Paris cycle race for charity. We were doing 80 miles a day, and everything was going fine until the last day, when I found myself without medication for a recurrent medical problem. The chain came off my bike, and so did I! I felt very dizzy, lost my vision, and couldn't even look up from the ground. But with only 10 miles to go I simply couldn't give up.

Although I was black and blue, bleeding and half-blind, I managed to persuade another rider to accompany me. The only problem then was that, although I knew the route, he didn't. So, we agreed that he would give me a running commentary on what he was seeing and I would tell him whether we should be going left, right or whatever. I never doubted that I could deal with the situation or thought that I might not finish. I don't know whether you'd call this resilience or just plain bloody-mindedness!'

As with the development of self-esteem, self-efficacy can be the product of positive childhood experiences – parents who actively nurture their children's ambition and who are role models for a 'can-do' attitude – or of negative ones. People who are forced by events to assume parental responsibility from an early age demonstrate competence way beyond their years. They realize just what is possible.

The Canadian-born social psychologist Albert Bandura found that self-efficacy, while often associated with particular personality types, can develop over time, and is inspired by one or more of the following four factors:

1   Personal experience – reviewing past successes, analyzing how your efforts contributed to the positive outcome and building confidence in your ability to achieve future success

2 Vicarious experience – looking at what others have achieved and feeling inspired to do the same.

3 Social persuasions – being convinced by others that you can achieve your objectives or deal effectively with problems

4 Physiological make-up – having the ability to overcome symptoms of stress or other physical limitations

Interestingly, when it comes to physiological factors, how we interpret them is probably of more significance than the symptoms themselves. For example, in a highly stressful situation, those with high self-efficacy are likely to attribute their fear and nausea to the importance of the occasion, whereas those with low self-efficacy are more likely to attribute such feelings to their own inability.

HOW TO DEVELOP SELF-ESTEEM AND SELF-EFFICACY

We have suggested in this chapter that self-esteem and self-efficacy can be developed, but how do you actually do it – how do you become that kind of person when it doesn't come naturally to you? How do you shift what is a pretty fundamental aspect of your personality?

Robert Dilts, a pioneer in the field of Neuro-Linguistic Programming (NLP), developed the logical levels model, which is a way of viewing an individual and analyzing their situation. It suggests that, in order to effect personal change, it is vital to understand the logical level at which the issue sits, and therefore how best to address it.

The logical levels model

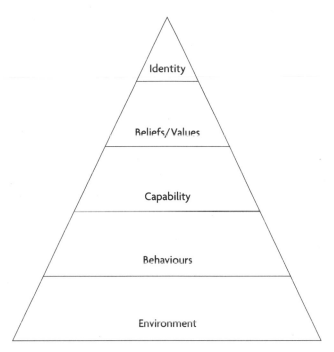

So, working up from the bottom:

- ENVIRONMENT is anything that is external to the individual, for example, other people's behaviour and the culture of the organization they work for
- BEHAVIOURS describe what an individual does or has done. It is the aspect of that person that others see
- CAPABILITY relates to an individual's skills, knowledge and core competence – it's what they *can* do
- BELIEFS/VALUES include the way the individual sees the world – what is important to them, their values, and the thoughts that drive their actions
- IDENTITY goes to the core of the individual. It is who they are

What we are talking about here sits right at the apex of the triangle – your identity. This, of course, is supported by your beliefs and values, which fuel the way you see yourself. These beliefs and values may be positive – which would be a trait in people with high levels of self-esteem and self-efficacy – or they may be negative, which would be indicative of lower levels. In order to build your self-esteem and self-efficacy, thereby boosting your overall resilience, you need to nourish yourself at the higher logical levels. This means demonstrating a sense of perspective.

Many people with a negative view of themselves look for evidence which supports this view. So, for example, when criticized for having said something insensitive (a one-off behaviour), they would interpret this as personal criticism – 'I knew they never liked me; I am stupid and indiscreet' – thoughts which sit at the identity level. The feedback is taken out of context. To build a positive view of yourself, it is important to look for evidence of success and work hard to get things in perspective, treating a minor setback as just that, a setback, not a permanent roadblock to development. Using this as your foundation, you might benefit from building your sense of self in terms of three key elements:

1   Self-awareness
2   Self-motivation
3   Self-affirmation

1 Self-awareness
You need to develop a realistic view of how other people perceive you, rather than relying on your own view of yourself and your capabilities, wherever that sits on the continuum ranging from self-deprecation (running yourself down) to self-

aggrandizement (bigging yourself up). This involves seeking feedback from those people whose judgement you trust as well as using empathy to anticipate other people's reactions to what you say – not least about yourself. For example, if you give the impression that you never take yourself seriously, why should anyone else do so? You also need to be clear about what you actually want from life, and what you're capable of. Self-awareness is the foundation stone on which self-esteem and self-efficacy rest. And, so long as your view of yourself is well-founded, the chances are that other people will describe you as well-grounded.

2 Self-motivation

Motivation is the force which causes a person to act in order to achieve a goal, and then to sustain that action until successful. Resilient people are self-starting; they don't rely on others to motivate them. While they might procrastinate a little, or reflect on the best way of approaching a task, they get on and do things, reasonably quickly. They can then sustain that action until the job is done. If you are not naturally like this – tending more towards prevarication than action – how do you curb these tendencies and become more self-motivating? There is no easy answer to this, but many people find that just taking a first step – any step – helps enormously.

3 Self-affirmation

In building self-esteem and self-efficacy, it is not enough merely to create success, you must also give yourself the credit for having done so. This calls for time and space to enjoy your own achievements, and to reflect on how you attained them. Constant 'sanity' and 'reality' checks are required along the way. And you should aim to become the supervisor of your own training and development programme. It's all about learning.

As mentioned earlier, you can ask others to give you feedback, but it's also important to get into the habit of doing this for yourself. Without this ability, you may find that you become dependent on others for your own positive view of self, which is all well and good until you either lose this external affirmation or the feedback is negative. Most members of the R-team describe themselves as their own harshest critic. One remarked that, although he still considers himself to be immensely competitive, it is himself he now feels in competition with. For him, a new 'personal best' has become the motivator, rather than other people's approval.

To demonstrate resilience, you require a combination of self-esteem and self-efficacy; this needs to be a fundamental part of your make-up – who you are. This grounding will enable you to take all the steps necessary to bounce back from tough times. However, as touched upon above, it is important that you get a sense of perspective on this – narcissism will be counterproductive. So too will a falsely elevated sense of what is possible coupled with a deluded view of your own importance – the 'great man syndrome'. Many of the worst corporate disasters occur when the person at the top of an organization comes to believe that they, and they alone, understand what needs to be done, and how. The complexity of modern life is such that this belief can never reflect reality. It is a toxic state of affairs when a leader demands blind obedience, silences all dissenting voices and puts in place the lethal combination of a skilful PR machine and a spineless Board!

So, there's a balance to strike. Both self-esteem and self-efficacy need to be well-grounded, and this means that your belief in yourself should be pitched at a level which is just higher than your current levels of competence. In talking to the R-team, we found that many seem to go out of their way to find new challenges, including some which they believe may be beyond them. This can lead to discomfort, or even symptoms of stress, but these abate as soon as they sense the possibility of achieving success. At this point, members of the R-team find that they return to their normal state of competence and confidence; they revert to their original 'shape', their belief that they can tackle pretty much anything life throws at them reinforced.

Chapter 4

Can do, will do - optimism and opportunism

Something's gone wrong — really wrong. What's your first thought? What's your initial reaction? What does your instinct tell you? Do you 'catastrophize', constructing a worst-case scenario and mapping out all the grisly consequences? Or are you instantly on the lookout for ways of reframing the situation, for your own and other people's benefit, in a way that transforms enforced change into an opportunity for improvement?

Our research highlighted optimism as a key marker of resilience; every member of the R-team described themselves as being optimistic, and the results of the NMRQ support this finding. One interviewee put it even more strongly: 'It is impossible to be resilient without being optimistic.'

WHAT IS OPTIMISM?

Optimism is about seeing the 'glass half full', about always looking for (and usually finding) the silver lining in even the darkest cloud. Optimism encourages people to feel positive about themselves, about other people and about the world's general direction of travel. Optimists believe that things are getting better all the time, and not necessarily just for themselves, but for others close to them and for society in general. Optimists are therefore likely to view change positively, and to be more confident about what the future holds – and that they will be able to cope with it.

Sales people are famous for their optimism, seeing each rejection as taking them one step closer to achieving their next sale. Contrast this with the concept of 'psychological conservatism', which is defined as anxiety in the face of uncertainty – 'I don't know what's going to happen next and because of that I'm very nervous'. Resilient people are generally positive, even happy-go-lucky; they usually thrive on uncertainty and the opportunities it brings.

> **'Yes, I am an optimist. I always believe that there is a solution, and that we can make things better.'**
>
> ....
>
> **'I find it hard to believe that I've got as far as I have. The position I hold and the money I earn seem bizarre to me. But I can't say it bothers me that much. Nor would it bother me if I lost it all.'**

WHY IS OPTIMISM IMPORTANT?

The benefits of optimism are not confined to building resilience. On the whole, optimists tend to be healthier and happier than their pessimistic cousins. Research in the Netherlands demonstrated that optimism actually reduces the risk of heart disease in men, and these findings were mirrored in 2009 in research on almost 100,000 women in the United States. Optimistic women were found to have a 9% lower risk of developing heart disease and a 14% lower risk of dying from any cause after more than eight years of follow-up. By contrast, their pessimistic counterparts – who tended to be hostile, distrusting and cynical — were 16% more likely to die over the same period. While there are thought to be chemical differences in the two types of people, optimists' ability to recover and bounce back is almost certainly linked to their tendency to take better care of themselves — to exercise more and eat healthily. Optimists can see the point of trying, and they believe there's a future worth trying for.

Research has also thrown some light on the role of optimism (or, rather, overoptimism) in marriage. According to research conducted by academics Ying-Ching Lin and Priya Raghubir in 2005, it seems that men are more optimistic than women that their marriage will be successful. This may be because men expect less from marriage than women, or it could just be a consequence of the finding that men are generally the more optimistic sex. Lin and Raghubir also found that women more often review the state of their marriage and, if necessary, reset their expectations of it. Men's views on the subject are less likely to change.

Aside from health and marriage, why is optimism so critical to resilience — to the ability to bounce back? Let's talk first about preparing yourself for the future. It helps to have a clear vision of the future, as a staging post between the present and wherever your personal 'time horizon' is located (some people are able to project their thinking much further forward than others). When this vision is strong, vivid and rounded, it's as if your brain and body subconsciously start working towards it — your 'inner programmes' take over. This means that you are much more likely to achieve success than people without vision. An optimist's vision is positive and encouraging, even idealistic at times. It helps the optimist to understand exactly where they are headed; it gives them a defined future to reach out for.

Optimism also gives you self-belief, a 'can-do' attitude and a positivity about the circumstances in which you find yourself. And positive thought inspires positive action. In this way, optimism is an energizing force, while pessimism tends to be a debilitating one. Energetic, upbeat and active, optimism is highly contagious – which means that others are motivated and encouraged too. The optimistic role model is very powerful.

Finally, optimists believe that there is always something to be learnt from bad experiences. They review the circumstances, taking a balanced view, which helps reduce the likelihood of making the same mistake in the future. The optimist has to find something positive in everything that happens to them, even really difficult stuff. For example, one of our interviewees, A, was with his desperately ill father just before he was due to leave on a very important business trip to China. His father told A that he had to go (and so he did), but as he stepped off the plane in Beijing he received the news that his father had died. Though personally devastated, A carried on with the trip, determined to do brilliantly well; once there – and with the knowledge that he could do no more for his father – he needed to take something positive from the experience. But it was not without a personal toll; although A felt pride in how well he had performed, he also felt guilt that he had been in Beijing rather than London.

PRAGMATIC OPTIMISM

'I'd call myself a pragmatic optimist.'

Optimism can be a powerful energizer when it is pragmatic. However, it also comes in two less desirable flavours – misplaced/blind optimism (based on fantasy rather than grounded in reality) and overdone optimism (a refusal to abandon a positive view when the evidence on which it was based turns out to be ill-founded).

Back in 2002, Diane Coutu of the *Harvard Business Review* described an example of pragmatic optimism (sometimes known as 'preparedness') in action — Morgan Stanley's approach to having offices in the South Tower of the World Trade Center. Morgan Stanley (a global financial services firm) realized that the iconic Twin Towers were potential terrorist targets well in advance of 9/11. Instead of thinking, 'It'll never happen — we'll be OK', they rigorously drilled their employees on how to evacuate in an emergency. On that fateful day, they succeeded in getting all but seven of their 2,700 employees out of the building.

Pragmatic optimism has three components:
1　Analysis of data
2　Creative thinking
3　Credible action

1 Analysis of data

There are two aspects involved in the analysis of data. The first involves the collection of information; the second, how you view it. One person diagnosed with cancer can be blindly optimistic, hoping and praying that all will be well, but doing nothing over and above that. Someone else might carry out research on the internet, talk to others who have been in the same situation, find out what action they can take to increase their chances of recovery — and then take that action. This is pragmatic optimism, because it is based on an assessment of risk and probability. Which approach is more likely to succeed?

Having collected your information (no matter how formally or informally you do it), there are always two ways to view it — positively or negatively. By nature, people tend to look for evidence which supports their preconceived ideas. In this way, pessimists have a habit of ignoring the positive information and seeing only the negative, whereas optimists do the opposite, filtering out the negative from the positive. Although they might be accused of viewing the world through 'rose-tinted spectacles', optimists are more likely to bounce back from tough times because they can see a positive route forward – and a way in which to get there.

2 Creative thinking

Complementing any analysis, creative thinking will help you view a situation in a way which may not be immediately obvious to others. For example, a couple we spoke to were unable to get employment in their chosen fields after one had been made redundant and the other had suffered an injury. They had come to the end of their savings and could no longer pay the mortgage. Quite by chance, they received an offer of free accommodation in France for a year if they renovated the house they stayed in. Both being optimists, they jumped at the chance, seizing the opportunity for their children to become fluent in French and for them to gain the skills needed to renovate properties. They thought that this could offer an alternative lifestyle for them, and that this experience would provide the ideal dry run.

Another couple we spoke to had a child who was physically and mentally disabled. As well as doing all they could to help the child, they also viewed what had happened as a 'gift', vowing that this would make them better, more unselfish, people. The situation strengthened both the family unit and the individual members within it.

Creative thinking also helps you to break issues down into their component parts, which not only makes them easier to deal with but helps ensure that the solutions you come up with genuinely resolve all aspects of the problem.

3 Credible action

You then need to turn your thoughts to credible action. There is rarely any point being optimistic when the world around you is laughing at your folly or gullibility; even quite plausible plans can fail because they lack credibility in the eyes of others If optimism needs to be well-founded, its products need to be well-sold. Why will others believe in your scheme? What relevant information or experience can you use to back up your ideas? What do you need to do to increase the plausibility of your plan, and get other people on board?

Making the sale

A senior IT project manager, M, wanted to transfer into a front office sales role - not a typical career move by any stretch of the imagination. She recognized that it was going to be difficult to persuade others to give her a chance, especially when there were many more qualified and experienced people than her in the business. So, she manoeuvred herself into project roles which required her to demonstrate her skills of influence and persuasion, roles in which it was of paramount importance for her to 'sell' her ideas to others. In this way, she developed a portfolio which was demonstrably sales-orientated. She also built strong relationships with the key people in front office and - after a while - started to seek their advice and secure their support for her transfer. She volunteered to help out on big proposals, to gain even more experience of the sales process.

After she had done all this, M took a proposition to the head of sales, in which the benefits of appointing her were clearly articulated. She had also thought through any potential risks and made recommendations for how these could be mitigated. She finished with 'next steps'. It was a very compelling 'sell' and, needless to say, she landed the job.

In summary, what we are talking about here is the ability to view things positively — not with blind innocence but *realistically* — and to take others with you.

WHO ARE THE OPTIMISTS?

Optimists tend to believe that they can make a real difference, that they can take positive action to influence events and circumstances. They tend to have what psychologists call an internal 'locus of control' — they, not outside events or influences, are responsible for, and can effect change (more about this later, page 64). Optimistic people have a positive, proactive attitude, which creates real results. As the playwright George Bernard Shaw remarked: 'The people who get on in this world are the people who get up and look for the circumstances they want and, if they can't find them, make them.'

But there are other elements at play here. People who are able to tolerate ambiguity also demonstrate optimism — they don't know what's going to happen, but they're OK about it. Taking this one stage further, maybe you count yourself among the ranks of the 'change junkies'. These are people who actively seek out change and, where there is none, create some! For these people, 'change for change's sake' is not necessarily the negative concept it is to many others. When a change is announced, they can only see the positives. Even when the change is ostensibly bad news, the change junkie will see the bright side. During the 2008 credit crunch and its aftermath, the optimists were those people who, when made redundant, appeared thrilled about the opportunities this presented. A few months later, these were the people who had started their own businesses, found other jobs or occupied themselves in a completely different way.

So, how optimistic are you? The questions below are taken

directly from the NMRQ. These are the questions that most accurately predict how optimism positively affects resilience. Work through the questions and rate yourself on a scale of 1 to 5, where 1 = I strongly disagree and 5 = I strongly agree. Then calculate your total score. It is important that you assess yourself honestly; if you know how genuinely optimistic you are (or not), you can then decide whether you need to change your outlook.

Optimism questionnaire

Question	Score
1 I have a positive mental attitude	3
2 I tend to bounce back from knocks	3
3 I can often create success from disaster	3
4 I am good at finding solutions to new problems	
5 In a difficult situation, my thoughts immediately turn to what can be done to put things right	
6 I've generally found that things turn out in an advantageous way for me	
7 I am good at seeing the silver lining	
8 I don't often envy other people	
Total score	

Interpreting your score

We found that the average score for this set of questions was 30, so those of you who score above this can count yourselves optimistic. A score of 24 or below means that there is definitely scope for you to look on the bright side more frequently.

But what if you don't score as highly as you'd like? Is optimism a personality trait that you either have or you don't have; or can you develop it? The good news is that we can all train ourselves to become more optimistic. Keep on reading to find out more.

LEARNED OPTIMISM

In 1975, the American clinical psychologist Martin Seligman coined the term 'learned helplessness' to describe the situation of animals (including humans) who, when faced with the realization that they cannot improve their position, eventually give up trying to do so. Even when the barriers to action are later lifted, the feeling of learned helplessness remains with them. It is one of the major presenting symptoms of clinical depression.

Some 15 years later, Seligman turned this idea on its head in a book called *Learned Optimism*. In this book, Seligman uses his understanding of what happens when people give up to suggest how they can instead formulate a more helpful and progressive mindset. More information about this process is given in Part 3.

WHAT IS OPPORTUNISM?

Opportunism is 'opportunity plus...' Confronted by even the blackest of clouds, the opportunist doesn't just see the silver lining, they use it to mint coins! Opportunism in the context of resilience is about identifying the opportunities that arise as a direct result of whatever has gone wrong. Linked with the creative thinking that enables the optimist to see things in a different light, opportunism is all about seeing how adversity can be turned to advantage – spotting the opportunity, and then making it happen.

Consider the following scenario. Your trusted nanny declares that she is leaving at the end of the month. The pessimist would go into a state of depression, certain that the children will react badly, and that the replacement will be inferior. The optimist would be certain that things will work out well – and take steps to ensure that they do. The opportunist would think about how the situation could be capitalized upon. They would see a chance to get someone even better in place. They might also decide that the time was right to switch from a nanny to an au pair, reducing their outgoings considerably and getting someone who would also do the cleaning and provide cover at all times.

At work, when redundancies are in the offing, the pessimist is deflated and downcast, certain that their head is going to be on the block. By contrast, the optimist feels confident that the value they add will protect them from the axe – and even if they are made redundant, that they'll have no difficulty finding a new position. The opportunist may go further, perhaps volunteering themselves for redundancy if the package is generous enough; they might even sell their services back to the company that has made them redundant (on a part-time basis, of course, while they set up their own business!). Winston Churchill put the difference succinctly: 'A pessimist sees the difficulty in every opportunity, an optimist sees the opportunity in every difficulty.'

The life stories of the R-team are full of examples of opportunism in action.

> 'The last time I changed jobs I did so because I had just finished leading a really successful, high-profile project; I thought my stock would never be higher. The whole process went so smoothly, it felt like an act of theatre.'

> 'There is always a way to get from here to there; you just need to be able to see the opportunity, to look beyond the here and now.'

So, we've talked about the kind of person you need to be if you want to benefit from high resilience levels, and also the outlook you need to have, which is where optimism and opportunism come in. We now turn to how resilient people actually behave.

Chapter 5

Leave it to me - taking control

The ability to take control of situations was the factor most frequently mentioned during our research into resilience. Almost everyone we spoke to said how important they thought it was to be in control of events, rather than to be at the mercy of other people's whims or circumstances they were powerless to affect. Being able to respond to changing events is at the heart of resilience.

One highly resilient woman, K, who had been left by the father of her two children, talked about the shock she had experienced when she discovered that he had been having a long-term affair with a woman 25 years his junior. Instead of talking about it – and attempting reconciliation – her partner had left that very same day. K could not influence the outcome in any way; it was a foregone conclusion, a decision imposed upon her. Apart from her obvious feelings of betrayal and devastation, her inability to exert any influence over events was one of the most difficult aspects of the whole experience. Over time, she started to come to terms with her partner's decision, and to take back some control, using the bargaining power she did possess to influence how things were going to be in the future.

The need to feel in control seems to be even more important in the workplace.

'It's very important for me to feel in control at work, though not necessarily to exercise it.'

....

'I recognize that I have to be in control, but as long as I am, I don't mind how difficult the task is.'

....

'Once you get to the top, you can concede - as long as you know you can take back control if you want to.'

There are two main aspects to taking control. The first relates to circumstances, the second to emotions.

CIRCUMSTANCES

Looking first at circumstances, if being in control is an important factor in determining levels of resilience, this might lead some to think that, in order to be resilient, you also need to be a megalomaniac – power-hungry and autocratic. But this is far from the case. Most of the people we interviewed drew a clear distinction between being in control and controlling. When we talk about control, we are not talking about micromanaging all aspects of a situation, or about being overly directing to the point of being dictatorial. Instead, taking control means:

- Quickly turning your attention to what can be done to remedy any problem
- Focusing on the positive actions required rather than how unfair or difficult a situation is
- Being proactive – not waiting for others to sort matters out for you
- Securing the necessary resources to put things right; delegating where appropriate
- Influencing others around to your way of thinking
- Being a positive role model

'In tough times, you need to try and focus on identifying the most important things that need doing, and where you can exert influence.'

'It used to be very important for me to be in control. I equated being in charge with things getting done, better! Now I'm more collaborative. My prime concern these days is building capability across the organization.'

The Jack Welch way

Jack Welch, former Chairman and CEO of General Electric (GE), used to say, 'Control your destiny or someone else will.' While this conviction underpinned his time at GE, Welch also realized that control need not necessarily mean 'command and control'; that command and control can stifle innovation, impair productivity and slow response times.

Having inherited a rigid, bureaucratic structure at GE, Welch set about streamlining the organization, cutting bureaucracy and peeling back red tape. He removed whole layers of management, empowering individual managers to take responsibility for their businesses. He energized others, encouraging learning and participation at all levels.

Although Welch garnered some criticism (his job-cutting could be quite ruthless), there is no doubt about the commercial success of his approach - his 20-year tenure at GE saw the company become one of the most valuable in the world.

LOCUS OF CONTROL

Our ability or desire to take control stems from what psychologists call our 'locus of control' ('locus' being the Latin word for place).

If you have an *external* locus of control, this means that you believe you are driven by external events and other people, and that, in reality, you have little influence over what happens. You tend to worry about events which are outside your control, complaining about how unfair things are and envying the 'good luck' of others. People with an external locus of control tend to become very reactive and negative, prone to whingeing and bitching about others. With only a finite amount of time and energy available to us all, these people inevitably achieve a lot less, and take far longer to bounce back from tough times.

By contrast, if you have an *internal* locus of control, you feel confident that you can exert significant influence over your own destiny, through your actions and beliefs. Your focus then is on what you *can* do to achieve a positive result, not on what you can't. People with an internal locus of control may say that they are lucky, but in reality they make their own luck. They are proactive and focused on making a difference. They spend their time and energy on reaching defined goals.

So, do you have an internal or an external locus of control? To get a better idea of this, you might be interested to know that there are significant clues to be found in the way you tend to think and use language. If you find yourself frequently thinking or saying things such as, 'This is hopeless', 'I can't believe this is happening to me', 'They've really got it in for me' or 'It'll never work', the chances are that – unless you are able to move on from this negative frame of mind relatively quickly – you have an external locus of control. Use of more positive language would indicate an internal locus of control.

Where you focus your time and energy also has a bearing. If you are energetic and active in terms of finding (and then implementing) solutions to problems, and in achieving defined goals, this indicates an internal locus of control. However, if you are someone who fails to define goals, who spends time worrying about things, procrastinates, and who prefers to complain about matters rather than take action to put them right, this indicates an external locus of control.

Complete the following questionnaire (putting a tick under either the 'yes' or 'no' column for each question) to see where your locus of control might lie.

Locus of control questionnaire

	Yes	No
1 Is there some bad habit, such as smoking, that you would like to break but can't?		
2 Do you take steps, such as exercise and diet, to control your weight and fitness?		
3 Do you believe that your personality was firmly laid down in childhood, so there's little you can do to change it?		
4 Do you make your own decisions, regardless of what other people say?		
5 Do you find it a waste of time to plan ahead because something always causes you to change direction?		
6 If something goes wrong, do you usually reckon it's your own fault rather than just bad luck?		
7 Are most of the things you do designed to please other people?		
8 Do you often feel you are the victim of outside forces you cannot control?		
9 Do you usually manage to resist being persuaded by other people's arguments?		
10 Are you sceptical about the extent to which your horoscope can tell you what you should do and what's going to happen to you?		
Score		

Interpreting your score

For questions 2, 4, 6, 9 and 10, score yourself two points for every 'yes' answer and zero for every 'no' answer. For the remaining questions – 1, 3, 5, 7 and 8 – score two points for every 'no' answer and zero for every 'yes' answer. Now calculate your score for each column, and then add these together. The maximum total score is 20, and the higher your score the greater the extent to which you take control of your life. Any score of 14 or above would suggest that you have an internal locus of control. Scoring below 14 suggests that you need to get a firmer grip on things; such a score may well indicate an external locus of control.

Whether you think you might have an internal or external locus of control, psychologists are divided as to whether locus of control is something innate – born into us – or whether it evolves as a result of experience; whether it's nature or nurture. Arguing that locus of control is preprogrammed is a swathe of academics who have found systematic shifts in locus of control through the lifespan. Typically, this might show that the locus is more external in adolescents (conjuring up images of teenagers shouting 'It's just not fair!'), then shifts towards a peak display of internal locus as we reach middle age. After middle age, the locus then shifts back to a more external bias. This model fits with the idea that people tend to become more and more confident and competent up to the power-wielding stages of their career (most leaders are at least over 40), then, as old age encroaches, tend to become less self-reliant and more critical of the world in which they live.

So, is the very nature of locus of control itself outside our control? Not at all. The idea that locus of control changes over a lifespan is a generalization over whole populations. It may not hold true on an individual basis, as evidenced by the existence of anyone who bucks the trend – and there are plenty of them! The locus of control is a mental construct, a personal philosophy; it can be changed as easily as thinking, 'Actually, I *can* do something about this'. And, according to our interviewees, the change can be made at an early age; many had started to turn their situation around during challenging childhoods. However, before we get into how to take control, or move its locus from external to internal, let's first explore why you should make the effort.

CONTROL AND RESILIENCE

One of the most basic reasons why taking control increases your resilience is that, if you are not in the driving seat, you will find it more difficult to reach the various levers you need to get back on course following a setback. Of course, as the following case study shows, you might think you are in control, but circumstances reveal otherwise!

All at sea

'I have a couple of examples about control, both taken from the same experience – sailing across the Atlantic as part of a small crew.

The first was when I realized that the skipper of the boat, who was a brilliant sailor but not a brilliant manager of people, was getting everyone's backs up. I confronted him about this, and told him he had to change his approach; we had to work as a team.

The skipper and I spent the next 18 hours not talking to one another (and trying desperately to avoid each other – difficult in such a confined space), until he finally apologized, addressed his shortcomings, and assumed real control.

My second example concerns an incident which occurred a little later, on my watch. We ran into a terrible storm, and I just lost it. I was ill and couldn't get my balance; I couldn't even distinguish between the sea and the sky. I was determined to complete my watch, however, to stay "in control". It took a 20-year-old to tell me to stop, to get my bearings and calm down.'

Refusing to take control, or considering yourself helpless, is a vicious and depressive circle that can be learnt, just as choosing to take control can also be learnt. In fact, Martin Seligman coined the term 'learned helplessness' (the idea that someone feels unable to exert influence or control, even when any obstacles to doing so have been removed, see page 58) to describe a marker of clinical depression. Taking control is also one of the best ways of boosting your self-confidence and optimism – key elements of resilience. But how do you do it?

HOW TO TAKE CONTROL

For most of us, our attitudes and beliefs determine our emotions, which in turn affect our behaviours; our behaviours then result in an outcome. The diagram below illustrates this cycle.

Attitudes, emotions, behaviours and outcomes model

OUTCOME
I fail to handle the situation well.
I let myself and the other person down

ATTITUDE
I really don't want to do this

BEHAVIOUR
I am short of breath.
I fail to make eye contact.
I don't come across as confident

EMOTION
I feel unnerved.
I feel underconfident

The reason the interaction between attitudes, emotions, behaviours and outcomes is described as a circle is that, nine times out of 10, the outcome you achieve will reinforce your original attitude. This attitude might be negative, or it might be positive. It's up to you to make sure it's the latter not the former.

A negative outcome

A young man, T, working in the media, thought that he was being discriminated against by his boss. All the interesting jobs seemed to go to his colleagues, and his boss barely spoke to him. T was failing to advance his career and feared he was going to get a poor appraisal, largely because he hadn't been given the opportunity to demonstrate what he was capable of.

T decided that he had to talk to his boss, but really wasn't looking forward to it. T's beliefs were, 'There's no point in talking to him. He's not going to listen and he'll probably penalize me further for giving him negative feedback. I'm dreading this conversation, and can't wait until it's over'. In terms of his emotions, T felt nervous, anxious, scared and underconfident. Not being a great actor, these emotions came through in his behaviour. He couldn't make eye contact with his boss, was inarticulate (even stammering from time to time), and found it very difficult to make his point succinctly. In fact, his boss didn't really understand what he was saying at all, just about recognizing that T had a complaint.

The outcome was not positive. T did not come across well, which reinforced the negative opinion his boss already held of him. In fact, his boss thought less well of him after the interaction than he did before, making him less, not more, likely to give T any of the interesting work in the future.

In order to make this cycle positive, T needed to turn his beliefs around so that they were far more positive. This would fuel positive emotions, which would come through in improved behaviour. In order to do this, he needed to use a technique called 'reframing'. Conceptually, reframing is a very simple technique, involving a three-stage process:

1   Being in touch with your attitudes and beliefs
2   Recognizing when your beliefs are negative or unconstructive
3   Immediately turning your beliefs around (ideally by 180°) so that they are positive

In this case, when T found himself thinking negative thoughts ('There's no point in talking to him', 'He's not going to listen', 'I'm dreading this' etc), he needed to turn this around at once. T would have achieved a far better result if he had thought to himself, 'There is every point in talking to him and, of course, he will listen – he's my boss'. To be even more effective, he also needed to prepare – 'How can I deliver the feedback in a constructive way, so that he does listen?' would be a far more helpful frame of mind than 'He's not going to listen'. Similarly, 'I can't wait until it's over' should be reframed as 'This is a great opportunity to engage with my boss and establish how I can support him more effectively'.

Of course, what you need to tell yourself in order to get a good, positive outcome will depend on the specific situation, but the basic principle is that positive thinking gets positive results. It helps you take control.

'When I'm playing a game of tennis, and it's not going well, I sometimes find myself thinking, "I'm going to lose". Unless I change my frame of mind pretty quickly, I do lose.'

'I think a real test comes when you are in the thrall of a bully, who undermines and belittles you. My education with this started early, when I had a really vindictive teacher at school. I remember thinking, "You bastard, you're not going to grind me down". I ended up not doing very well in his subject, but it wasn't because I felt intimidated or bad about myself.'

Reframing is not a new idea; the power of positive thinking has been around since the 1960s. However, people often find it difficult to put into practice. One challenge is cultural. This type of technique seems to come far more readily to Americans than it does to many Europeans. Some European cultures are quite cynical; individuals are 'trained' to manage their expectations down (so that they are not disappointed) rather than talking themselves up. The difficulty with this approach is that negative thinking achieves negative results. If you find yourself thinking, 'We probably won't win this contract', or 'I don't think I'll get a good mark in my exam', or even 'This film is going to be really boring', the chances are you won't be 'disappointed'. So, the first challenge is to overcome the cynicism and give it a go.

The second challenge often involves changing the habits of a lifetime. Not an easy proposition! One individual we worked with was an extreme example of this. Whatever happened, no matter how objectively positive the event was, he always saw the negative. This was so deeply engrained in his personality that it had affected his physiognomy. His face looked perpetually miserable and the corners of his mouth turned down, even when he was smiling. His challenge was not small. He needed to reframe his thinking literally hundreds of times a day in order to bring about real change.

This links to the third challenge – the discipline required to effect personal change. If, by nature, you have an external locus of control, and tend to react negatively, the good news is that this is not a life sentence. You can change it. However, it does take real discipline – on a daily basis – to do so.

EMOTIONS

Research on resilience points towards a high positive correlation with 'emotional intelligence' – you are more likely to be resilient if you are also emotionally intelligent. Emotional intelligence was a concept developed by the American psychologist and journalist Daniel Goleman in his bestselling book of the same name, published back in 1995. Broadly speaking, in order to score highly in terms of emotional intelligence, you need to demonstrate five attributes:

1 Being in tune with your own emotions
2 Self-regulation of your emotions
3 Self-confidence
4 The ability to empathize with other people's emotions
5 Strong interpersonal skills

Self-awareness and flexibility run implicitly through all five categories, and 'self-regulation' is a core component in itself. Control of your emotions is key. This doesn't mean to say, however, that resilient people are automatons, completely buttoned up, seemingly devoid of feeling. Indeed, our research with highly resilient people identified a significant percentage who admitted 'losing it' from time to time. However, the vast majority felt that they did tend to be more in control of their emotions. They succeeded in achieving a balance between airing their grievances and going into meltdown.

> 'It is very important to feel in control of myself.
> I try and cultivate a calm approach, while
> injecting pace and urgency when necessary.'
>
> 'When I lose control, I try to take a step back. The key is
> to gather your thoughts, to start communicating some
> positive messages. Sometimes it's helpful to literally
> remove yourself from the situation for a while.'

If resilience is about bouncing back from tough times, it is vital that you have some outlet for your thoughts and feelings – but that outlet must be appropriate, both in terms of whom you talk to and how you do it (this is covered in more depth in Chapter 9). Losing control can have a negative impact on your ability to bounce back. Many people find that the embarrassment of having lost control lasts far longer than the problem that caused them to do this in the first place. They beat themselves up, agonize over how they should have handled the situation, and struggle to get events into perspective.

Still, it is important to recognize that changing your response can be difficult; some people are just more fiery than others. They have a short fuse. If this is you, how do you change? With great difficulty is the simple answer. However, if you reflect on the attitudes, emotions, behaviours and outcomes model on page 68, you will appreciate that, if you control your attitudes and beliefs, you have a far better chance of controlling your emotions. Reframing, therefore, not only has an impact on your ability to influence events around you, but also on your ability to self-regulate.

Of course, there are many other tactics that people employ to help them keep control, none of which will be new to you, but which nonetheless are highly effective. Taking a deep breath, counting to 10, doing some exercise or writing an angry email (but not sending it) are all ways that can help you achieve this. If, having tried all of this, you still find you are prone to the odd outburst, remember that this is actually healthier than bottling things up and brooding on issues for months on end. But it is important to move on; apologize where necessary, but don't beat yourself up. As one of our interviewees remarked: 'A second ago is history and you can't change it. You can only think about how to put things right now.'

Chapter 6

No worries - dealing with stress and anxiety

If *resilience* is about bouncing back, regaining your original shape after having been pulled in all directions, *stress* is a force which, if not handled well, can seriously distort you – temporarily or permanently. The ability to identify, and then deal effectively with, stress is a key characteristic of resilient people.

WHAT IS STRESS?

Up to a certain level, stress is a positive, motivational force – an energizer which encourages us to act, to confront issues and achieve. Dr Hans Selye, a pioneer in the study of stress, discovered that stress differs from other physical responses in that its effect is the same regardless of whether the stimulus is positive or negative. In other words, you can experience the same feeling whether you receive good news or bad. The physiological symptoms of nervousness are exactly the same as those of excitement. Selye termed negative stress 'distress', while he coined the term 'eustress' to describe the stress that motivates and inspires us. On the Yerkes–Dodson curve (see overleaf), eustress represents the point at which stress levels and performance increase simultaneously. Eustress is useful, beneficial, and even good for our health.

The Yerkes-Dodson curve

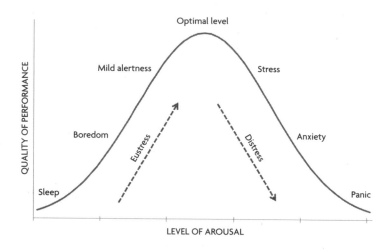

As individuals, it would be very helpful if we knew the exact point at which our *eustress* tips over into *distress*, but, unfortunately life doesn't organize itself so conveniently. We all have different tipping points, in the same way that we are all stressed by different things and react in different ways. However, it is fair to say that those who are highly resilient manage stress better than others; they take it in their stride. Most of the resilient people we interviewed liked being kept busy – juggling different priorities, remaining active in order to achieve what they achieve. If anything, they were more comfortable with having a bit too much to handle than with a relaxed, doable workload.

One interviewee recognized the force of this. In his first couple of years at college he got involved in practically everything – sport, music, the union – and did well in his exams. In his final year, he decided that he needed to concentrate on his studies, but he couldn't really focus. His explanation for this was that he is 'designed to work at full tilt – like my Lexus hybrid – which really needs to be driven regularly or it loses its power!'

Interestingly, many of the resilient people we interviewed appear to take so much in their stride that they believe themselves to be stress-free, although to others, looking on, they seem to be operating under immense stress.

Indeed, it is very unusual for these people to be debilitated by stress, and in the rare circumstances when it does happen, they understand how to minimize its effects (see page 84). Instead of being weakened by stress, these people actually find that:

- Crisis brings out the best in them
- They are able to turn disaster into success, and have confidence in their ability to do so; they are not ground down by stressful situations
- They take control because they're confident and secure, turning their thoughts immediately to what can be done to put things right and fully expecting a positive outcome
- They are curious, which means that they try different things. They understand that there are risks in not taking risks

It's not just that the tipping point of these individuals is greater than most people's, their reaction to stress is also different.

STRESS-PRONE PERSONALITIES

It has long been believed that certain personality types are more prone to the negative effects of stress than others. American cardiologists Ray H Rosenman and Meyer Friedman were the first to categorize people as being either 'Type A' or 'Type B'. Type A people are highly competitive, impatient, always on the go, driven types, whose main aim in life is to win. By contrast, Type B personalities are laid back and relaxed; they are more likely to seek (and listen to) the input of others, and tend to take one thing at a time.

The 'instant stress detector' below has been modified from the work of Professor Cary Cooper of Lancaster University, who extracted a short checklist from a much longer questionnaire on behaviour and heart disease. The detector will help you determine whether you are more likely to be Type A or Type B. Tick one box in each row.

Instant stress detector

1 Are you casual about appointments		Or never late?	
2 Are you uncompetitive		Or very competitive?	
3 Are you never rushed		Or always rushed?	
4 Can you wait patiently		Or are you impatient?	
5 Do you take things one at a time		Or do you try to do lots of things at once?	
6 Are you easy-going		Or are you hard-driving?	
7 Do you assume the best in others		Or do you at times feel hostile?	
8 Are you generally positive about others		Or are you generally critical of others?	
9 Are you pragmatic		Or are you a perfectionist?	
10 Are you a good listener		Or do you often interrupt?	
11 Do you usually express your feelings		Or do you tend to hide your feelings?	
12 Do you find it easy to relax		Or do you find it difficult to relax?	

Interpreting your score

The more ticks you have in the boxes in the right-hand column, the more likely you are to exhibit Type A behaviour.

Psychologists debate the usefulness of this Type A, Type B categorization, which was initially developed to predict an individual's likelihood of developing heart disease and other stress-related illnesses. The argument continues as to whether there is any merit in the theory, with Type As typically adamant that the disparaging descriptions of their approach must have been written by Type Bs, whom they accuse of being jealous about all the stuff they (the Type As) have achieved in their lives! For their part, self-rated Type Bs suggest that Type As must be deeply insecure and in need of medication, and so on. Regardless of the technical quality of this tool, it has endured for more than 30 years, and still sparks lively debate. There's clearly something in it.

When it comes to stress, the dilemma for Type As is that, while they have a great many positive characteristics, they are more prone to generating negative stress for themselves, but generally less well equipped to deal with it. They can suffer as a consequence. The challenge for Type As, therefore, is to retain the positive aspects of their approach to life while reducing (or even eliminating) the more destructive elements.

Although the R team as a whole tends towards the Type A personality, individual members within in it appear to cope immensely well with stress. They rarely allow stress to disrupt their lives and the achievement of their goals.

So, what makes them different? If you look back to the instant stress detector, you will notice that some of the boxes are shaded. These are the Type A traits which our research has indicated are more destructive than the others – traits which our interviewees have all modified or overcome. Take perfectionism, for example. Several members of the R-team told us that, in the early years of their career, they were harshly critical of anything less than 100% performance – in others as well as themselves. Over the years, however, they have chilled out a little, becoming more comfortable with concepts such as 'fit for purpose' or '80/20' (otherwise known as 'Pareto's law', where roughly 80% of effects come from 20% of causes). Now they only look for perfection on the rare occasions when nothing less will do. Members of the R-team also tend not to feel hostile towards (or blame) other people. In fact, they are more likely to compete against themselves, ensuring that they are the best they possibly can be.

The members of the R-team have all recognized the value that involving others can bring; they minimize their stress levels by sharing the workload, delegating effectively and leveraging teamwork.

> **'You need to have an open disposition; you need to be able to inspire trust and invest trust in others. Taking risks with people pays off; they're always capable of contributing more.'**
>
> ....
>
> **'Delegation is really the only way you can make life work, so you'd better be good at it!'**

Members of the R-team tend to demonstrate more empathy and pragmatism than most Type As, although one or two expressed frustration with other people when they complained about stress, suggesting that they 'just needed to get on with it'.

Other divergences from the classic Type A personality include:

- Recognizing the importance of rest and 'downtime'
- Listening to others and giving them the benefit of the doubt
- Getting things into perspective

- Understanding that, nine times out of 10, pragmatism will win over perfectionism

All these qualities are very important when it comes to personal resilience. But what about the Type Bs?

Since we have seen that the Type B personality leads to a 'healthier' response to stress, it is perhaps Type Bs, rather than Type As, that we should be seeking to emulate. Moreover, Lydia Temoshok and other psychologists have extended the Type A, Type B theory and suggest that there is a third type – Type C – where C stands for 'Cancer-prone'.

These psyhcologists claim that an over-representation of patients suffering from cancer exhibited the reverse of Type A personalities, particularly the suppression of emotions (including anger) and the adoption of a passive, eager-to-please attitude. Where Type A behaviours cause an intense 'fight or flight' response that puts strain on the cardiovascular system, Type Cs may suppress this response, but then experience a more intense second phase stress response which suppresses the immune system and may be associated with developing cancer.

This gives rise to the following model:

Stress response model

←――――――――――――――――――――――――――→

Type A	Type B	Type C
'Arousal' stress response	'Healthy' stress response	'Immune-suppressing' stress response

If you are Type B, the implication is that you are more moderate, that you have a sense of competition but are not driven to win at any cost. It implies that you are generous in your dealings with others and demonstrate a high degree of emotional intelligence. You are relaxed, pragmatic and have a healthy sense of perspective.

Regardless of personal categorization, it is fair to say that we all need to demonstrate these kinds of behaviours if we want to manage our stress levels and bounce back from tough times. Knowing what is likely to stress you out, anticipating challenging situations, managing your reactions and dealing with any symptoms of stress are all critical skills.

STRESSORS

'Stressors' are the causes of stress. Medically speaking, this can be anything which requires you to adapt or change – in any way. The key is to identify what is likely to cause you negative stress, and to develop strategies to ensure that your personal tipping point from *eustress* to *distress* is as high as possible – and that when you do occasionally tip over, you can deal with it.

There are so many potential stressors that it's barely worth itemizing them; it could be anything. Some are global – death, marriage, moving house, childbirth, and so on. Some, however, are more personal, and these are the ones that vary hugely. For example, some people are stressed by having too much to do, others by having too little. Some loathe uncertainty and find themselves enormously stressed when plans are unclear; others thrive on ambiguity and feel straitjacketed by undue regulation.

Research into the causes of stress at work indicates that incompatibility with your boss, and being a 'round peg in a square hole', come at the top of the list. So, a careful choice of job and boss (where possible) are two of the most effective ways of reducing your risk at work. The consequences of not so doing can be painful.

A poor fit

Having worked very happily in my job for many years, my organization - a well-known and respected charity, which had been in existence for almost 100 years - was unexpectedly taken over by a large corporate. Our charitable status disappeared practically overnight, along with our name and identity. We became part of a faceless monolith.

Unhappy with their new situation and the culture of the new organization, many of my colleagues left as soon as they could. Those of us who remained felt marginalized and disenfranchised; we just didn't seem to fit anymore.

To make matters worse, the new organization knew very little about my particular area of activity and, eventually, I was made redundant. Demoralized, and to an extent traumatized, I found myself out of work aged 40.

Although I had the opportunity to go freelance, my caution got the better of me, and I ended up accepting another full-time role. Whereas my work at the charity had been varied, stimulating and collaborative, this new role was narrow, restricting and isolating. It was also extremely process-driven, which I was not used to, and which I didn't much like.

Although, in theory, I had the technical skills to do the job, I just couldn't seem to get to grips with it. I did not enjoy the work, nor the joyless atmosphere. I became depressed, and started to exhibit physical signs of stress. My performance (which had never been great) deteriorated. After a while, I realized that I was just not cut out for this particular job, and eventually made the decision to leave, a difficult lesson learnt.

When it comes to stress, what is vitally important is that you understand exactly what is likely to cause you negative stress – at quite a detailed level – and that you become good at anticipating when any of your personal 'fuses' is in danger of being ignited.

HOW TO MANAGE STRESS

In broad terms, managing your stress effectively involves either removing the causes of stress or dealing as well as you can with the symptoms.

There are two possible strategies to achieve this, which are distinct, but which can both be brought to bear on the same issue. The first involves *distraction*, the second involves *resolution*. Before exploring these, it's worth noting that, when it comes to dealing with stressful problems, some people don't even want to engage in debate unless a solution is possible; for them, it's just not worth the airtime. However, the other important consideration is, of course, the nature of the stressor – there are some issues you just can't crack straightaway. For these, you might want to employ a distraction strategy.

Distraction

There's no doubt that many people have the capacity to get worked up over issues which seem hugely worrying when they're wrestling with them but which, on reflection, appear much less threatening. Resilient people know that things have a habit of working out, no matter how difficult they are at the time. Unlike many of us, they use this knowledge to eliminate symptoms of stress; to borrow an old Second World War slogan, they 'Keep calm and carry on'. Distraction involves removing yourself from a situation, giving yourself some space, which allows you to get some perspective on a matter, and minimize your reaction to stress. Sleep, exercise, taking proper holidays, writing things down, breathing deeply and talking to others are all thought to be immensely helpful in reducing or eliminating the effects of stress. Allied to this is the ability to pace yourself, to know when to rest and when to go the extra mile.

> **'When I'm very stressed I try to put off important decisions, realizing I'm not in a fit state to make them.'**

> **'I tend to be very productive for a few days and then get a bit lethargic. At that point I force myself to do something small but constructive – for example, doing the household bills.'**

> **'I've got much better at saying "no", and not feeling under pressure to meet all demands (including answering emails) immediately.'**

Sometimes, even classic Type As can grasp the importance of pacing themselves, though they might need a little outside help!

In their 1997 book *Golf Beats Us All*, Joseph A Amato and Robert L McMasters describe how big tournaments can bring out the nerves in even the most experienced golfer. A player's skill, confidence and coordination can fall to pieces; they can barely keep a drive on the fairway. This was the case with Greg Norman who, having held a commanding lead for the first three rounds of the 1996 Masters, seemingly buckled under the strain, losing by a substantial margin to Nick Faldo on the final day. It hadn't always been like this, however, as the authors note:

'A master caddie from the American tour, Pete Bender, is reported [in *Golf* magazine] to have saved an earlier tournament for Greg Norman. Holding a three-stroke lead on that last day of the 1986 British Open, Norman snap-hooked his drive off the sixth tee. Bender grabbed Norman by the shirt and said to him: "Look, Greg, you're playing too quick, and you've got to slow down. You're the best player in the field. You're going to win this tournament if you take your time and enjoy it and don't press the issue." Norman slowed his pace and won the tournament by five strokes.'

Resolution

As its name implies, resolution involves analyzing the cause of a problem and establishing a solution. This sounds very straightforward, but is rarely so simple in reality. There is often a need to break the problem down into much smaller chunks and deal with each, one by one. This has the dual positive effect of dealing with the problem – albeit probably quite slowly – *and* making you feel as though you are taking some kind of action.

In our research with members of the R-team, we found that they tend to be 'contra-agglomerators'. Agglomeration is where, under stress, unconnected and trivial issues become part of one immense, insurmountable and complex problem. People who demonstrate high levels of resilience, then, are very good at dissecting complex issues, understanding the component parts and then dealing with these individually, rather than combining them into one impossible problem.

> 'I'm a great one for making lists - what needs to be done this year, this quarter, this month.'

> 'I tend to deal with things in batches because the more I'm on top of something the better I feel. If you're faced with a problem that is too difficult - you're probably in the wrong job!'

COGNITIVE BEHAVIOURAL THERAPY

But how about those who are less well equipped to deal with stress than the R-team? For these people, distress can lead to anxiety and depression. If you are feeling very anxious and low, you may need to seek a medical consultation. However, instead of being prescribed a course of antidepressants, you might find your doctor recommending Cognitive Behavioural Therapy (CBT).

CBT is an umbrella term for a range of psychological techniques that can teach people to recognize, minimize or even eradicate the types of thoughts that cause distress. It posits that the majority of people's problems are created by themselves; it is not necessarily the situation itself that is stressful but the way in which the person in that situation perceives it. Thus, by breaking down those perceptions and assumptions, the anxiety can be overcome without further interventions. CBT teaches people to remain 'in the present', believing that stress is only caused by worrying about the future or the past, rather than the here and now. Patients are sometimes set 'worry times' — periods of the day when they deliberately worry, rather than letting it spill over into the rest of their lives. This time could be in the morning, after the kids have left for school, or on the commute home. It could be when you go to the gym or take a run in the park.

Other tactics include talking through a set or worries and then challenging them one at a time. Asking a very distressed person repeated questions about what is bothering them, and why, will often throw up some catastrophic 'possible' outcomes that are actually not very realistic. For example, not having revised enough for a particular exam could provoke concern about failure, permanent unemployment or social ostracism. However, on challenging these assumptions, the person can come to recognize that, even if one of these outcomes did come to pass, it wouldn't necessarily lead to catastrophe (for example, millions of people without qualifications are employed, popular etc). Moreover, they may accept that the first event is relatively unlikely to happen – they might drop a grade rather than fail the whole test.

The success of CBT as an intervention will be determined over the coming years, but there are already two factors in its favour. First, there is growing evidence that CBT is more effective (and more cost-effective) than prescription drugs. Secondly, there is evidence that the methods work when delivered by a computer program, thus reducing the need for qualified practitioners, and enabling people to seek help over the internet without risking the stigma still associated by some with having a mental illness. However, the evidence for CBT's superior performance over other treatments is not yet conclusive; you should still talk to a qualified doctor if you feel this type of therapy might be of use to you or someone you know.

In therapy

J grew up with a schizophrenic stepfather, who was abusive and violent. J got into the habit of watching for signals or triggers, and anticipating her stepfather's moods, so that she was able to avoid situations likely to make him angry. For example, if one of her siblings started winding him up, she would make sure that the 'offending' individual was removed immediately. This put her in the habit of anticipating what could happen and taking actions, large and small, either to avoid difficulties or to enhance her ability to bounce back if they were unavoidable.

Later in life, as a mother, she experienced a few problems with her own children. For example, both her children were excluded from school. However, J's ability to anticipate (and deal with) difficult issues helped ensure that the bad times were short-lived.

Fortunately, J managed to pick up a few different strategies through a project she volunteered for at her work. The project was wide-ranging, and involved mastering a variety of coping mechanisms, including CBT. J found that she could use the techniques of CBT to manage both her children's issues and her own, the thinking process assisting in the analysis and subsequent resolution of difficult issues. Staying in the 'here and now', J asked herself CBT-type questions, which helped her to dissect problems, test her assumptions, and get things into perspective, avoiding catastrophic fantasies. She did the same with her children (very subtly) which helped them arrive at their own solutions, and ultimately enabled them to turn a corner in their lives. J continues to use CBT techniques on a regular basis.

Chapter 7

I'll be the judge of that - making decisions, cutting losses

We can all make decisions. We do it thousands of times every day — whether it's to push the snooze button, turn the temperature up on the shower, wear blue or black socks, brake or accelerate on our approach to an amber light, and so on. The ability to make timely, high-quality decisions is part of everyday life. And if you're worried about making bad decisions, spare a thought for the other end of the decision-making continuum — indecision. As the Spanish philosopher Maimonides put it 900 years ago: 'Indecision causes opportunities to be missed, progress to be delayed and a considerable embarrassment of its own, once the hesitation has been uncovered.'

MAKING DECISIONS

Members of the R-team tend to adopt a common approach to decision-making. But before sharing this with you, first complete the following quiz to help identify your own style.

Listed overleaf are pairs of statements (statements 'A' and 'B') describing how individuals go about making important decisions. Review each of the statements and, for each pair, circle the letter of the statement that you believe is closer to your style of decision-making. In many cases, you may feel neither the A nor the B statement fits you exactly; in this case, select the response you would be more likely to use.

Decision-making questionnaire

1	I plan my important decisions carefully	A
	I put off making many decisions because thinking about them makes me feel uneasy	B
2	I generally make decisions which feel right to me	A
	I generally make decisions on the basis of logic and data	B
3	I double-check my information sources to be sure I have the right facts before making decisions	A
	I don't do a great deal of research when making decisions	B
4	When I make a decision it is more important for me to feel the decision is right than to have a rational reason for it	A
	When I make a decision it is more important for me to have a rational reason for it than to feel the decision is right	B
5	When I make a decision I trust my inner feelings and reactions	A
	I often procrastinate when it comes to making important decisions	B
6	I often need the assistance of other people when making important decisions	A
	I prefer it when others make the decision	B
7	I often make impulsive decisions	A
	I talk to a lot of people to inform my decisions, to try and secure their buy-in	B
8	If I have input from others, it is easier for me to make important decisions	A
	Seeking input from others complicates the decision-making process	B
9	I rarely make important decisions without consulting other people	A
	I prefer to make important decisions myself	B
10	When making decisions, I do what seems natural at the moment	A
	I would prefer not to take a decision at all than make the wrong one	B

Score sheet

Review your responses to the questions and circle your choices on the table below. Once you have done this, add up how many you have circled in each column.

	1 Rational	2 Consultative	3 Intuitive	4 Independent	5 Avoidant
1	A				B
2	B		A		
3	A		B		
4	B		A		
5			A		B
6		A			B
7		B		A	
8		A		B	
9		A		B	
10				A	B
Total					

Interpreting your score

The maximum in each category is 4, which is clearly a very high score; 3 is high, 2 is average, while 1 is low and 0 very low. But beyond this, what do the scores mean?

First, it is important to explore the extent to which you are *avoidant*. Do you struggle with some decisions, tending towards procrastination and delaying the moment at which the choice needs to be made? Or would you always prefer to make a decision, no matter how little information is available or what the implications of that decision might be? If you relate more to the first statement, the chances are your avoidant score will be high. If, by contrast, you relate more to the second statement, avoidance is unlikely to be a problem for you. Your avoidant score is given in column 5. As mentioned above, a score of 3 or above is a high score. If your avoidant score falls into this category, you need to consider the implications. Are there times when it would be better to grasp the nettle and actually make a decision – even if that decision may not be perfect? Might this avoid a great deal of procrastination, and possibly stress, on your part?

Once you have established the extent to which you are avoidant, you then need to consider the nature of the decisions you make. There are two axes along which most people can place themselves, the rational–intuitive and the independent–consultative.

Decision-making axes

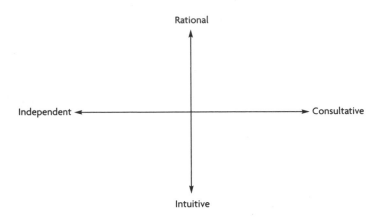

As with the avoidant scale, a high score on any one of these axes is 3 or 4. If you have a high *rational* score, you probably adopt an analytical, logical approach to decision-making. The chances are, you think long and hard about the criteria you are going to apply, and then work methodically through these. You are able to stand back from decisions and take a dispassionate view. You try to avoid getting sucked into emotional debates; for you, these muddy the water and prevent people from seeing clearly and objectively. By contrast, if you are high on the *intuitive* scale, you are more likely to go with your gut feeling. If you apply any criteria at all, they are probably intuitive, rather than rational – driven by values and emotions. Your heart, not your head, is in charge.

On the independent–consultative axis, those with an *independent* streak make their decisions on their own. They rarely seek the input of others, preferring instead to demonstrate what they consider to be strength of character and leadership qualities. They know their own minds and are not afraid to stand by decisions. Conversely, a high *consultative* score indicates someone who values the input of others, who actively seeks their opinions and is likely to listen to any advice given. To their mind, this not only makes for better decisions but also ensures that others buy in to the chosen course of action.

When scoring the decision-making questionnaire, some people may find that they have average scores on all five scales. This could suggest someone with an approach that changes according to the situation they face at the time. However, it might not indicate a positive result at all. The individual might, instead, be someone who wavers, who finds it difficult to make up their mind, and who could end up choosing the wrong approach time after time. If this is you, challenge yourself. Do you get it right most of the time, or not?

It is more common for someone to get one strong score on each of the two axes. For example, one person might be highly rational and independent, while another is almost entirely intuitive and consultative. Clearly, how you score on these axes – and your thoughts about how you could improve your decision-making – will affect how you respond to any advice given in these pages.

However, if you can bear in mind your natural bias, you will get more out of what follows. But before we get into that, let's find out what members of the R-team do when it comes to making decisions.

DECISION-MAKING PATTERNS

Our research with the members of the R-team established a clear pattern to their decision-making. Resilient people tend to be instinctive, intuitive and quick decision-makers (only one member of the R-team believed they were a rational decision-maker). Resilient people are rarely avoidant and don't dither, except – interestingly – on trivial matters; many of our interviewees admitted to taking important decisions quickly, but to procrastinating when it came to deciding what shirt to wear or what to have for lunch! Despite being intuitive, many said that, once they had reached their conclusion, they might well test it out by gathering data and conducting analysis.

Historically, members of the R-team have been highly independent decision-makers. However, over time, they have come to realize the importance of seeking the input of others – that there is worth in other opinions – and that differences as well as similarities are to be valued. So, as well as collecting data to test out their intuition, they also talk to other people. This usually serves to reinforce their initial judgement, but it can sometimes cause them to shift their thinking.

Often, it's less about changing their mind than getting others on board – securing their commitment. After all, it's all very well making the 'right' decision, but if you're to get other people to accept your ideas, you have to seek – and listen to – their opinions. This doesn't necessarily mean that you are obliged to act in accordance with their wishes, but it does mean you need to deal appropriately with any contrary views, ideally winning adversaries over to your way of thinking and accommodating differences. After all, as Dale Carnegie pointed out many years ago: 'There is only one way to get anybody to do anything, and that is by making the other person want to do it.'

> 'I've learnt that it's better to spend time bringing people with you, and indeed encouraging them to believe they have been involved in making the decision. However, you very rarely get everyone to agree with you. You then need resilience to force through your view in the face of some opposition.'

Flexibility was a recurrent theme to emerge from our research, and this was displayed in the R-team's approach to decision-making.

> 'I firmly believe that perfection is the enemy of the good; you have to take reasonable risks.'

The ability to change your mind – and even to make the occasional U-turn – was also highlighted as being critical to the resilient decision-maker. This ability was generally seen as a strength rather than a weakness. Resilient people recognize that it often takes a great deal of courage to change your mind.

> 'Over the years, I've come to realize that changing your mind isn't necessarily a bad thing. In fact, you lose more credibility by sticking to bad decisions.'

HOW TO IMPROVE DECISION-MAKING

Resilient people tend not to procrastinate. Their 'avoidant' score is therefore low. This is linked to personality – resilient people are optimistic, they demonstrate self-efficacy and take control of situations. They make judgements and take decisions; they are not avoidant. If this doesn't sound like you, you need to do something about it. What exactly you need to do will differ from person to person. For some, it will involve taking soundings, seeking input. For others, using problem-solving or analytical thinking tools might be the answer. And for yet others, it might just come down to taking a risk, asking yourself, 'What actually *is* the worst-case scenario?' 'Is it really worth all this prevarication?' 'What would be the first step?' 'Can I do it now?'

So, once you've decided to act, what is the best way of making a decision? The somewhat indecisive answer to this question is, it depends – on the nature and importance of the issue, and on the people you're dealing with. Despite the fact that most members of the R-team tend to be intuitive decision-makers by inclination, they acknowledge that flexibility of approach is critical. Sometimes it is essential to do the due diligence, to collect all the data and analyze the information properly – when choosing which firm should build your new kitchen, for example, or what course you want to study at college. You might have an instinct about this, but your decision must bear scrutiny. At other times, you need to trust your intuition – whether it's choosing who your life partner will be at one end of the scale, or what to wear to the office party at the other. Your decision-making style just needs to be appropriate.

So, in terms of becoming a better, more resilient decision-maker, some need to hone their powers of intuition, while others need to develop a more rational approach. These are covered below.

Becoming more intuitive

As we have established, resilient people tend to be intuitive decision-makers, and they become more intuitive over time. This stands to reason – intuition grows with experience, and experience develops as you do. Confidence in your instincts and judgement also grows over time as you achieve positive results or outcomes, as you are proved right.

But it is worth remembering that, at one level, we are all intuitive decision-makers. Going back to an example cited earlier in this chapter — deciding whether to brake or accelerate on the approach to an amber light — we don't analyze all the available data, conduct a risk—benefit analysis, generate a range of possible options and then decide which option to take, based on a list of predetermined criteria. That would be impossible, not to mention insane! No, we just make a snap judgement and then do it.

But there's more to it than that. The unconscious parts of our brains process a far larger amount of information than we can consciously register. Take David Beckham's World Cup-qualifying free kick against Greece in 2002. Researchers at three universities collaborated to investigate the physics behind 'bending it like Beckham'. Beckham has only a moment in which to strike the ball, but the computer program the researchers developed needed several hours to perform the necessary computations to predict the ball's flight. In this case, Beckham isn't relying on science so much as on a lifetime of experience and practice — the hours spent out on the field, come rain or shine, perfecting his craft.

The same applies to all of us. Many of the skills we possess — driving a car or playing the piano, for instance — are all conscious processes to begin with, demanding massive concentration and thought as we learn. This continues until we've mastered the skill, at which point it becomes automatic. So, one of the best ways to increase your unconscious processing is through practice and gaining experience. To accelerate this process — and help develop confidence in your instincts – there are a number of 'psychological shortcuts' you can employ. These shortcuts normally serve you well, but on occasion they can skew your judgement. Once you have an appreciation of these risks, you can become more aware of when these shortcuts are helpful, and when they are not. Five key shortcuts are summarized below.

1 Availability
   The availability shortcut describes how people make decisions based on the information that springs most readily to mind, because of personal experience or publicity, for example. In this way, when asked to say whether a 90-year-old woman would be better off living with her daughter or in a nursing home, a third party might base their decision on what suits their own mother, or the recommendations of a report they have recently read, rather than the needs of the woman in question.

2 Anchoring and adjustment
   Anchoring and adjustment suggests that people's decisions are influenced by information that has been most recently presented, whether or not this information is relevant. This sets the 'anchor' or starting point. The final decision then tends to be a minor adjustment from the anchor. So, if you wanted to sell a painting to an antiques dealer, the price they initially offer you might set the anchor, and the price you finally decide to accept will then be based on this.

3 Framing
   Related to anchoring and availability, the framing shortcut concerns the way in which relevant information is positioned, and how this can influence the outcome of a decision. Of particular relevance is whether the information is presented in a positive or negative light, and whether it involves any

potential loss to the decision-maker. Research indicates that most of us are irrationally biased towards avoiding potential losses at all costs, even when taking a risk is likely to yield high returns.

4   **Statistical inferences**

Not everyone feels comfortable when required to handle statistical problems in an abstract manner, and there are three ways in which this can skew decision-making. The first is that we tend to favour a high *absolute* outcome over a high *relative* outcome. For example, more people will choose 'Lottery A' with nine winning tickets than they will 'Lottery B', which has only one winning ticket, even if the percentage chances of winning Lottery B are higher. The second is that we are better at working with frequencies than we are with percentages. So, for example, a teacher asked to estimate how many of her class are likely to pass a particular exam would probably be able to provide an actual number, but might struggle with the percentage that the number represents. And the third (known as 'baseline versus salient') is that we tend to attach greater weight to information we consider to be salient (or 'in our face') than we do to information which objectively has more relevance. For example, when buying a car, many people are more influenced by a friend's opinion than a scientifically-conducted consumer survey.

5   **Sunk cost**

This describes the way in which some people 'throw good money after bad', simply because to abandon the project feels like a total waste of their investment. Even though they know that the additional spend won't achieve the objective, they still desire that particular outcome, and continue to work towards it.

When you find yourself instinctively leaning towards a particular decision, question why you are doing so. Are any of these shortcuts at play? And, if so, is it appropriate that they are, or would you be better off eliminating the bias? Understanding this will help you to develop your judgement, and become more confident in your intuition.

Improving your sense of intuition can also be a matter of relearning how to listen to the signals your own body is sending you. We are all aware of the 'sinking', 'low' or 'heavy' feelings of having taken a wrong decision. These are manifestations of actual physical processes, such as increased muscular tension, reduced endorphins and nagging thoughts. Contrast this with when you feel you've made the right choice. At these times, you probably feel 'light', 'tall' and 'relaxed'.

The next time you are happy with a decision you've made, notice how you're feeling and what your body is doing. Then, when you're nervous about a choice you are faced with, try to mimic the posture and frame of mind you had in this previous situation. This will give you greater conviction and more confidence in pushing through the decision you've made.

Becoming more rational

So far we have focused on becoming more intuitive because we have found that resilient people tend to take decisions in this way. However, as mentioned earlier, the R-team also advocates a flexible approach, appropriate for particular circumstances, which might mean adopting more of a rational stance at times. If you are largely intuitive in your decision-making, you might need to hone your ability to be more rational. As with intuition, this too can be developed.

Peter Drucker, the well-known writer and management guru, devised a rational decision-making process, with six stages as follows:

1   Define the problem/opportunity
2   Analyze the problem/opportunity
3   Develop alternative solutions
4   Decide on the best solution
5   Convert decisions into effective actions
6   Evaluate and control

It's probably fair to say that – whether you're naturally a rational decision-maker or not – these stages are actually common sense, and little explanation is needed. However, the problem with this process, as with many like it, is that if you are a rational decision-maker you probably go through a version of this anyway (whether you're aware that you're doing it or not), and if you are more of an emotional decision-maker it's unlikely to appeal to you. It seems dull and uninteresting – you feel it won't produce a solution you really believe in. So, for those of you stifling a yawn, let's see how this process can work in practice.

In analysis

Two organizations merged, which meant that a number of senior roles were duplicated.

Raj was a highly respected leader in one of the organizations, who was tipped to go to the top. However, post-merger, his counterpart David was awarded the senior job, and Raj was required to report to him. David wasn't thought to be especially competent, and he wasn't particularly good with people either; it was not a popular decision. Raj found himself essentially having to do David's job, but not getting any of the credit or reward for it. This put him in a real dilemma - should he leave the organization or stick with it, trusting that he would ultimately get what he deserved?

Raj's judgement was clouded by emotion and damaged pride; he really couldn't work out what to do. After several unhappy months, he decided to try and adopt a more rational, analytical approach – not his natural style at all. The first challenge was to define the problem; this turned out be far more difficult than it first appeared. After much head-scratching and soul-searching, Raj decided that the central issue was whether he still had a future with the organization – and whether he wanted it.

In terms of his analysis, Raj concluded that the main factors were:

- The decision was the wrong one

- His pride was damaged

- He had no respect for David, especially since he wasn't performing in the role

- This meant that he lost some respect for the senior management who had taken the decision to appoint David

- He was essentially doing much of the job that David should be doing

- Senior management hadn't made much effort to explain their decision, or to appease him

- He had no sense of a future with the organization

Having gone through this analysis, Raj was surprised to find that his main cause of dissatisfaction was the fact that his bosses hadn't communicated effectively with him. Nor had they given him any sense of the impact of David's appointment on his future career. Having been seen as a rising star, Raj felt as though he'd been unceremoniously dropped.

The next stage of the process was to develop a range of solutions. Based on his analysis so far, Raj came up with a number of options – he could:

- Tolerate the status quo

- Resign

- Have an open and focused conversation with senior management about career opportunities

Tolerating the status quo was out of the question; the current situation was making Raj stressed and demoralized. While resignation was a possibility, he figured that he could always do that later. So, he opted to have an open and focused conversation with senior management, and set up a meeting. In preparing for this, he needed to establish clear objectives, which were to:

- Give senior management some constructive feedback

- Explore his career options – sideways or upwards

- Be clear and assertive about what he wanted

Raj was pleased about how the meeting went. He received the reassurance he so badly needed and was surprised to discover that the decision to appoint David had been a political one. While no immediate promises were forthcoming, it was made clear to Raj that, if he was patient and remained a positive influence, he would be rewarded with a role that suited his talents.

Many false promises are made in business, and so Raj wasn't holding his breath, but he felt somewhat better anyway. And, in this particular case, his faith was rewarded; after a few months Raj was promoted into another department. Looking back, Raj had to concede that, had he not gone through this rational decision-making process, he wouldn't have had the constructive conversation with management, and would have become increasingly bitter and negative. He would not have achieved the promotion he so strongly desired.

CUTTING YOUR LOSSES

As a postscript, we should mention one specific type of decision we all face regularly, and about which members of the R-team have diverging views – the decision whether (and when) to cut your losses. Former Federal Reserve Chairman Paul Volcker attributes the financier George Soros' phenomenal success in investments to him being wise enough to quit when still ahead of the game. Although Soros was capable of cutting his losses, the process wasn't painless: 'I often used to get backache due to the fact that I was wrong. When you're wrong, you have to [either] fight or take flight. When I make the decision the backache goes away.'

Members of the R-team also reported some discomfort. As one interviewee remarked: 'I'm not good at cutting my losses. I always believe I can fix things. It goes against the grain to quit.'

Sometimes, of course (and despite your best efforts), you have to admit defeat; you need to recognize when something's just not working.

> **'When I discover I've made a bad decision, my instinct is always to try and rectify it. If this is not possible, then I do move on; I have no problem taking responsibility for the mistake.'**

So, should cutting your losses be a rational decision or an intuitive one? As with many of these things, views differ. Some believe that a rational approach is best – once you weigh up the body of evidence in an objective, dispassionate manner the answer will become clear. Others argue that you need to go with your gut feel. Does this seem right? Is it likely ever to work out or should you pull the plug? Both rational and intuitive approaches are appropriate, but in different circumstances. The only safe assumption to make, therefore, is that you should do both – analyze the issue rationally and also use your intuition. You can then compare the results. If the results are the same, then the decision is clear. However, if they are not the same, you might need to employ different tactics. Ask other people. Carry out additional research. Whatever methods you use, in order to be genuinely resilient, you need to know when to quit.

This highlights a potential conflict in the highly resilient personality. Optimism argues in favour of persevering – 'Surely I can do it?' – while pragmatism says, 'Why bother?' But this kind of dilemma doesn't detain the highly resilient for long. They'll cut their losses when they have to, and they rarely waste time revisiting a decision once it has been made – or remade.

Chapter 8

Getting better all the time –
lifelong learning

There's no question about it, resilient people learn – from their mistakes, from their successes, and from other people. This is something that, for many of the R-team, they picked up in childhood. It seems as though, from a very early age, members of the R-team resolved to avoid the problems of the past. Those with difficult parents said that they wanted above all not to be like them, whereas anyone who had suffered from poverty or hostility was determined that their own families would enjoy security, stability and harmony.

These findings mirror previous research. The sociologist Emmy Werner, of the University of California, found that around a third of severely disadvantaged children were unaffected (even at the time) by the deprivation, alcoholism and abuse they were surrounded by. Of the remaining two thirds, many got into trouble during their teenage years, frequently turning to petty crime. But by the time they reached their 30s and 40s, they had turned themselves around, clearly determined not to repeat the mistakes of their parents.

It appears that resilient people respond proactively and crea-tively to troubles, using the experience to strengthen, rather than undermine, their self-esteem. It is a positive cycle – if you take positive learning from things that have gone wrong for you, this not only boosts your self-esteem but also your self-efficacy — your belief in yourself and your ability to succeed. What is more, learning will help increase your optimism — you will have more faith that things can and will work out in the future, and the knowledge to maximize the chances that they do. Your sense of being in control of your own destiny also increases. The mere fact that you are learning from your mistakes increases your resilience. It becomes a virtuous circle — the more you learn, the more resilient you become. Lessons learnt early in life, whether at home or work, can stand you in good stead.

LEARNING FROM MISTAKES

You've probably been encouraged throughout your life to learn from your mistakes. Research has clearly demonstrated that we learn more when we make a mistake than we do if our first attempt is correct; the element of surprise in discovering we are wrong encourages learning. Psychologists from the University of Exeter have even been able to measure how quickly this happens. Their research has established that there is an early warning system, a mechanism in the brain, which takes just 0.1 seconds to react to things that have resulted in error in the past. This demonstrates that we all learn from our mistakes, but resilient people may just do so more than their less resilient counterparts.

> 'For me, the only purpose of mistakes is to learn from them. If you don't do that, it's a complete waste of time and energy! You need to unpick it to improve it.'

> 'When I've gone out to learn a new skill, I've generally done it pretty thoroughly and really immersed myself - forcing myself to do the task that I've got wrong again and again until I get it right.'

Starting out

'Fresh from college, I was determined to get a job in publishing, preferably book publishing. I knew it was a very competitive field – particularly for editorial work – but my heart was set on it.

Although I had no direct prior experience, I managed to secure a number of interviews. When I was finally offered a job, however, it was for a magazine, not a book, publisher. Running short of funds, and having been encouraged to "take anything in publishing" just to get my foot in the door, I accepted.

The work turned out to be quite technical, not at all creative like I imagined. It was also my first full-time role, and I lacked confidence as well as experience.

Keen to show my employers that I knew what I was doing, I failed to ask some key questions about how the magazine worked. I made a number of easily avoidable, but serious, mistakes. As a result, I lost the job.

Although I was devastated by this turn of events, I remembered the words of a friend from college, "You always mess up your first job".

When I had initially heard this, I thought it sounded very defeatist. But now that this had actually happened, I discerned a different, ore positive, meaning. While I was very sorry to have failed, my friend's remark helped me realize that maybe my experience was not uncommon; that you tend to make many, many mistakes in your first job, but that you can learn from this. I realized that my mistake had been not to speak up early enough when I did not understand something, fearing my questioning would be interpreted as ineptitude.

Armed with this new insight, and with my friend's remark ringing in my ears, I quickly signed on with some publishing agencies. I soon secured another position, but this time I made sure I spoke up when required. I spent five happy years there.'

HOW TO LEARN

There are a number of different ways in which you can learn, including from your mistakes. Some of the most effective are covered below.

Conduct a post-mortem

A classic way to evaluate what's happened is to conduct a post-mortem. What actually went wrong? What caused the problem? What other factors influenced events? Who was involved? What were the processes? A post-mortem can be formal or informal. It can be carried out in a group setting (with the other people involved) or alone.

Interestingly, members of the R-team were somewhat polarized on this subject. The majority believe passionately in the value of the post-mortem and conduct them rigorously, while a small minority believe that it's far more important to move on from errors – as rapidly as is decently possible.

> **'I often conduct post-mortems, although only on what I could have done differently.'**

> **'When dealing with negative feedback, the safest thing to do is to assume that there is some truth in what's been said, rather than pointing the finger and rubbishing the person who offered it.'**

> **'I'm not much of a one for post-mortems. I tend to think, "Nobody's dead, let's move on".'**

> **'Looking back mustn't prevent you from moving forward.'**

When you review the past, it is important not to get bogged down in the 'blame game', but to focus on the genuine learning. This is important; there is reviewing mistakes and reviewing mistakes! Say, for example, you are a member of a cycling group. Nine of you decide to go on a cycling tour together over the summer, but things don't work out quite as planned. A mistake with the accommodation (a vital email had not been received) means that some members of the group are forced to share a budget bedroom with no air-con, while others have the run of a lovely, cool apartment; tempers flare, 'friendships' are tested. How do you react, once safely back home? On the one hand, you *could* conduct a full analysis of how awful things were, who said what, who was to blame, the embarrassment caused, the disastrous consequences, what you wished hadn't happened, how many of the group will probably never speak to you again, and so on. And then dwell on the answers to these questions, without really moving on.

Many people torture themselves in this way, but this is not learning. It may even inhibit your ability to bounce back, thus reducing resilience. The positive alternative still involves analyzing what went wrong — otherwise it would be difficult to learn from mistakes — but in a more constructive, future orientated way. Maybe you learn that you always need to ring ahead to confirm arrangements rather than rely on email. Maybe you recognize that, in a group of this size, there will almost always be personality clashes and different agendas, and that these become more obvious when you are in each other's company 24/7. This is practical, experiential learning; learning that you can take forward in your life, and not just on holiday!

In the workplace, a post-mortem often takes the form of a meeting, facilitated by a member of the team or an outsider, at which all aspects of the situation are analyzed. Again, this should not come from the perspective of apportioning blame, but of focusing on the future.

It was the British ad man, Robin Wight, who pioneered the approach known as 'interrogating your problems'. Wight's argument was that, although it's usually painful when a serious mistake is made (it wastes time and money, and makes everyone miserable), you can turn the situation on its head by conducting a post-mortem so rigorous that it becomes almost impossible to make the same mistake again. It can actually be motivating – as well as useful learning – to 'take revenge' on a problem. Here's a way to do it.

The positive review process

Before conducting any post-mortem, you must first make sure that you are in a receptive *frame of mind*. Remember, your objective is to answer some critical questions:

- What do you need to do in the future to make sure this type of mistake doesn't happen again?
- What were the positives in the experience, and how can you learn from them?

● How can you grow from this experience?

Having a receptive frame of mind means having a healthy sense of perspective — 'It really isn't the end of the world'. It involves being optimistic — 'There's bound to be a silver lining, I just need to find it'. You also need real determination to make the most of what's happened. Being in tune with your thinking, and then turning it around whenever it's negative or unconstructive (ideally by 180°), will assist enormously in the learning process. It will put you in the right frame of mind, enabling you to see things from different — and more positive — perspectives, and allowing you to take control of your future.

Having the right mindset is important because change is difficult. Think about it. What is your *motivation* to change? Many less resilient people make the same mistakes over and over again. This is often because there's no real incentive for them to do things differently. You need immense self-awareness to understand both what will drive you to make the change and what's holding you back. Research has clearly indicated that there are usually 'positive by-products' associated with an unwanted behaviour, and until you plan how you can replace these with equally valuable alternatives, your chances of making a successful change are slight.

Take giving up smoking as an example. Most people see smoking as a nasty, dirty habit, including many smokers! But it must offer some positives, otherwise nobody would do it. Failing to kick the habit is as much down to these positive by-products as it is to the incredible addictiveness of the drug. So, smokers might say that they do it because: it relaxes them (even though it's a stimulant), it's social, it's how they get to find out what's going on, it forces them to take breaks during the working day, it's a sign of non-conformity, it's cool, it reminds them of when they were young, or whatever. Some dedicated smokers can fill pages! But, inevitably, some of these reasons will be more important than others. Identifying the most important by-products, and planning alternative ways to satisfy these needs once the smoking is gone, will enhance your chances of success.

More broadly, you also need a clear understanding of what generally motivates you. When you have succeeded in making a change, what was the incentive? What drove you to persevere?

Once you are in the right frame of mind, and have established how you are going to motivate yourself to change, you are then in a position where you can start *learning*, and then *review* (see page 119).

Think or talk things through

Many people like to reflect alone. They calmly analyze the facts of a situation, in an objective manner, without allowing emotion to cloud their judgement. Some people find that it helps to write everything down, perhaps under headings, continually asking the question, 'What can I learn from this?' They might believe that – when the matter is something professional rather than personal – this is the method for them. Others, however, recognize the benefits of talking things through, either with those who have been directly involved in the issue or with someone more impartial. This could be a trusted confidant or a friend; or it could be a coach or counsellor, someone who will help them understand the events of the past and what they can learn from them for the future.

According to James Flaherty (the author of several influential books on coaching), as well as dealing with any current issues, a coach should always aim to leave the coachee self-corrective and self-generative. In this way, the individual benefits from increased self-awareness, with the ability to analyze events in the moment and alter their course of action accordingly. They also have a real focus on their future development.

Be mindful

Two professors at the University of Michigan, Karl Weick and Kathleen Sutcliffe, have conducted significant research in organizations where human life is perpetually at stake — nuclear power stations, emergency hospital departments, the military, airports and the like. They refer to these as 'high-reliability organizations', not because mistakes don't get made but because the public trust them to provide a good level of service no matter what the circumstances — in other words, they must be resilient.

Weick and Sutcliffe summarize the required mentality of these organizations as being 'mindful'; they are fixated with failure as a means of improvement. Air traffic controllers do not regard a near miss as a lucky escape, rather they analyze the circumstances ruthlessly to establish how the incident happened, and — as a consequence — how it could be avoided in the future. Whenever a plane crashes, the 'black box' is always a high priority for the search team, not so they can start dishing the blame but so they can learn from the experience. Resilient organizations also think about possible future failures, and any decisions reflect the need to reduce the likelihood of such events occurring. Mindfulness allows the significance of a small error to be more apparent, and the appropriate, vigorous response to be taken.

Role model

Another method of learning, successfully employed by many people, is known as 'role-modelling'. This involves isolating a specific skill that you want to master, and then identifying someone you know who does it brilliantly well. You then have a choice. You can either observe the other person and try to emulate their behaviour or, better still, you can interview them. The idea here is to ask the individual a battery of questions aimed at getting inside their head and understanding exactly what they are thinking, feeling and taking note of as they are preparing for (and then doing) whatever it is that they do so well. This exercise can sometimes have surprising results.

A female partner in a law firm was interviewed about her ability to 'work the room' by someone who really struggled with any form of networking. This individual had had a number of experiences which he had found embarrassing, and wanted to learn the secrets of this partner's success. To his surprise, he found that the partner hadn't always been good at networking. In fact, she suffered from acute shyness. This, however, was part of her success; because she knew how difficult networking was, and could empathize with anyone who seemed to be having problems talking to others, she was determined to go and help them, overcoming her own personal barriers in the process. This knowledge inspired the individual to try and do the same. It transformed both his attitude and his performance; he now no longer struggles at these types of networking events.

Conduct research

Apart from conducting a post-mortem, being mindful, thinking things through, talking things through and modelling others, there are other ways of learning. Take the woman who was diagnosed with breast cancer and then conducted an extensive research exercise to learn exactly what she needed to do in order to maximize her chances of recovery and survival. She read avidly – everything she could lay her hands on – and then explored the various options to establish which advice was the most relevant and reliable. Or the woman who, when told she and her husband would never have children, investigated the matter so thoroughly that — without any medical training — she helped pioneer an operation to reverse her partner's 'infertility'. They ended up having four children! Use the internet, read books, talk to experts, attend seminars, sign up to courses — do whatever it takes to inform yourself as well as you can.

AND FINALLY

Once you have implemented any course of action, you then need to *review* how effective it's been; this is an essential part of the learning process. It may well be that your first attempt (or even your second, third or fourth) is unsuccessful. You must then use all the techniques and resources outlined above to review why this is. Is it because you're not actually motivated to change — at some level you don't really want to? Or is it because you're lacking in a critical skill? Maybe it's just that the circumstances are not right at the moment. There are many reasons why your initial efforts might have been unsuccessful; it's just a question of working out what these are and planning to address them.

If, by contrast, your efforts have been successful, it is vitally important to acknowledge this, and to give yourself credit for having changed. It is remarkable how few people actually do this as a matter of course; as a result, many still hold views about themselves which are more negative than they should be — they don't give themselves the recognition they deserve. And without this, they harbour historical perceptions and the learning process is incomplete.

Hitting rock bottom

Following a series of traumas in his personal life, S entered a period of self-destructive chaos. He started drinking way too much, and occasionally driving while drunk. His work suffered, since he was regularly hungover in the office; his job was becoming increasingly untenable.

Despite having a long-term partner, S fell into a series of affairs, and spent most of his time with people who were clearly not good for him, neglecting those who really cared. He was suffering from low self-esteem, and hurting himself badly – almost punishing himself. Inevitably, these relationships didn't work out. One by one his new playmates drifted away, while his partner started distancing herself. He became very isolated.

S was on the verge of losing everything; he had hit rock bottom.

Reaching an all-time low was the wake-up call S needed; he resolved to take control of his life. For S, it was really important to understand how he had got into this bad space and, indeed, *why* he had got there. S did some of this soul-searching on his own, just reflecting and trying to work out why things had gone so horribly wrong, but he also sought support from a therapist. This was very valuable in helping him understand the causes of his behaviour and extracting the learning. But, probably most importantly, S found that his old friends were still very much there for him. This helped him to rebuild his self-esteem and start to value himself again, halting the negative spiral in which he had found himself. Self-reflection, counselling and support from friends combined to create a powerful learning experience.

Ten years on, S has managed to avoid being dragged down again. While no longer in counselling, he still uses the techniques he learnt there to help him grow and develop.

Chapter 9

With a little help from my friends - making the most of other people

Many of the people we interviewed for this book believe that resilience is the key distinguishing characteristic of successful people, along with a clear understanding of the implications, and obligations, of accepting that 'the buck stops here'.

Being individually accountable certainly seems to be a key component of resilience. However, there is also a strong belief that, in order to cope with (and bounce back from) tough times, you need to involve others. Resilience requires you to strike a balance between going it alone and relying on other people, between healthy competition and cooperation. Certainly, the support of others at times of great difficulty is extremely helpful. By contrast, lack of support – and the accompanying feelings of isolation and uncertainty – can seriously undermine your psychological wellbeing and levels of resilience.

One place where this is dangerously common is at the very top of many organizations. Offering the boss constructive criticism takes considerable courage, while being overheard praising him or her won't necessarily endear you to your colleagues. So, feedback and support tend to be in short supply among those who have to make some of the most difficult decisions. This explains the growing tendency of very senior people to use executive coaches, not just because they need an objective sounding board but also to find out what others really think of them, and to support them in their responsiblities.

> 'Resilience is certainly enhanced by having a supportive team, but [if you are a leader] ultimately you always carry the can.'

Sticking together

In 2009, during the initial spread of 'swine flu', a group of female tourists saw their holiday of a lifetime transformed into a terrifying ordeal. The women had been allowed to check in to a Hong Kong hotel, despite the fact that a guest had been rushed to hospital with the virus shortly before they arrived.

Less than 24 hours later, half the group were locked into the hotel. The other half were locked out - without passports, a change of clothes or any means of survival. Those inside the hotel were quarantined, with only contaminated tap water to drink. Two of their party, however, were taken to separate hospitals, where they were kept in freezing decontamination chambers, without clothes or food. They underwent horrific testing, that took them months to recover from.

As for the women who were barred from the hotel, they had nowhere to go, and no means of checking in to another hotel. Fortunately, one of them had friends on the island who were able to put them up. But things were about to get worse. Despite the fact that they had been refused entry to the hotel, the women found themselves branded as 'fugitives' in the press, and described as being 'on the run'. The police were sent in to round them up. The women feared incarceration in a Chinese prison, but were instead taken back to the hotel, where things weren't much better. They were still locked in their own rooms, forbidden to see one another. Their sense of isolation was intense.

Being resourceful, and having access to mobile phones, the group managed to draw their plight to the attention of the world's media, who then lobbied for the women to be given fresh water to drink and to be allowed to move from room to room, so they were at least able to talk to one another.

Once this permission was granted, the group vowed that the only way they would get through this experience would be to do everything as a team. And that's exactly what they did. The group took decisions - and actions - collectively. Although they weren't together the whole time, the support network they created was powerful and empowering, protecting them against the worst effects of psychological distress.

As well as having a negative effect on psychological wellbeing, going it alone can also be bad for our physical health. Sometimes we need a major jolt to wake us up to this fact. Take the example of one of our interviewees who had been advised by doctors that his habit of absorbing pressure, and confiding in no one at work, may have played a significant part in his contracting a rare form of cancer. Since none of the alternative triggers to the condition appeared to apply, the individual accepted the suggestion. He has been at pains to modify his behaviour now that he is back at work, following successful treatment.

Operating in isolation can also have adverse behavioural implications. Talking issues through with other people provides an opportunity to get things into perspective; refusing to do so, however, provides an opportunity for things to get out of proportion, or even to acquire paranoid beliefs. In tough times, it is tempting to start finger-pointing; to blame others for your problems and to question the motives behind what they are saying or doing. Without the chance to air or discuss such concerns, or to test their validity, we become prone to suspicion and anxiety. These negative feelings inevitably undermine our self-confidence and willingness to trust others; attributes that underpin our powers of resilience.

WHY IS NETWORKING DIFFICULT?

In our work as coaches, we are frequently asked to help individuals build support networks.

It is surprising how many people find this a daunting prospect, and how many different reasons they find for not addressing their relationship-building skills! For example, they say they don't want to:

- Lay themselves open to others, particularly if their levels of trust are low
- Demonstrate what they perceive to be weakness
- Be a burden on others
- Take up the valuable time of others
- Make themselves look stupid or incompetent
- Raise false hopes in others
- Risk rejection

Your personality type will have a bearing on how easy or difficult you find it to open up to (and benefit from) other people. This is less of a challenge for extroverts, who are used to voicing their opinions and airing their feelings. Extroverts are unconcerned about 'wearing their heart on their sleeve', about asking others for assistance, or, indeed, being asked for help by others. They are 'people-hungry', prone to being bored by their own company. As a result, they are only too eager to master whatever techniques oil the wheels of social discourse.

Introverts are just the opposite – more reflective by nature, uncomfortable in large, noisy gatherings, and happy to think things through alone. They don't have a compulsion to verbalize and share their thinking in the way extroverts do; opening up feels risky to the introvert, and they are more reluctant to ask for support. To the confirmed introvert, the suggestion that they should devote time and energy to creating and sustaining a formal network of useful contacts feels uncomfortable, not to say unnatural.

ARE YOU A NATURAL NETWORKER?

Are you the sort of person who always 'knows a man who can'? Or are you someone who observes networking activity with a mixture of distaste and envy, wondering where on earth people have managed to drag contacts up from? Answer the following questions to see if networking comes naturally to you. Place a tick in either the 'true' or 'false' column against each statement.

Networking questionnaire

	True	False
1 I am quick to pick up the phone		
2 I like to work things out for myself		
3 I always read about who's doing what in the paper or on the web		
4 I prefer to email people rather than phone them		
5 I'm not scared to ask for support from people		
6 I'm always introducing people to each other		
7 My daily contact with people is limited to a few close colleagues		
8 At parties, I'm always fascinated to hear about what others do		
9 I feel uncomfortable asking for favours		
10 I would describe myself as an introvert		
Score		

Interpreting your score

For questions 1, 3, 5, 6 and 8, score two points for every 'true' answer and zero for every 'false' answer. For the remaining questions – 2, 4, 7, 9 and 10 – score two points for every 'false' answer and zero for 'true' answers. Calculate your score for each column, then add these together.

The maximum total score for this short test is 20, and if you are anywhere near this mark, you are a true networker. In fact, any score above 14 is quite high. A total of 6 to 12 is OK, but you should examine any statement for which you scored zero, and think about the implications. A score of 4 or below suggests that networking is really not your thing at all. However, even the most introverted person can make progress in this area – provided they want to, and as long as they do it in a way that is consistent with their personality and values.

WHAT DO YOU NEED?

Regardless of whether you are a natural networker or not, the art of enlisting other people to advance your cause, or to help you bounce back from tough times, is something which can be developed. But you need to be clear about exactly what you're looking for. At the most basic level, just having a sympathetic ear – a confidant – can help you to get things off your chest. Beyond this, however, others can act as a sounding board; they can help you get things into perspective, reassure you, provide critical (ie honest and objective) feedback, facilitate learning (both from their own experience and by helping you recognize lessons in your own) and provide opportunities.

A sympathetic ear

Earlier in this chapter, we talked about personality (see page

124). We made the point that, by nature, extroverts are generally much more comfortable opening up than introverts. However, regardless of how natural or unnatural disclosure may feel, it is a fact that airing issues can accelerate recovery from trauma. Expressing your thoughts and feelings also enhances resilience.

Sometimes, all the other person needs to do is listen. The mere process of talking can provide release; it can act as a safety valve. Whether it's at work, home or down the gym, it is important to identify a safe place to talk. 'A problem shared is a problem halved' may have become a cliché, but science confirms that merely giving voice to our concerns – identifying our emotions and problems, and also possible 'roadblocks' to resolution – can have therapeutic value.

A word of warning, however; when you share your problems with others be sure to choose your confidant well. Are you sure you can trust the individual? What will the effect be if you do offload to that person? Take the example of the senior executive we worked with recently who bottled up issues as a matter of course, until they became so intense that he felt the need to download – to anyone who would listen, in groups of people if necessary, and usually in an inappropriate way. While this acted as a safety valve of sorts, the high-flyer usually felt so embarrassed afterwards that the exercise was counterproductive. He learnt that he needed to choose his moments more carefully, and had to work on his method of delivery. He had tended to operate at one or other extreme of a continuum – he was either totally inscrutable (which was the norm) or, once he opened up, he revealed literally everything about himself.

Self-disclosure is an important part of relationship-building, but it's crucial to get the timing and the volume of what you reveal about yourself right: too much too soon is as much of a turn-off as a refusal to release any significant details about yourself at all.

Once you have chosen a confidant, you need to make sure that they understand their role in your life. A confidant will be someone with whom you can discuss sensitive issues, issues you (and they) will not be sharing with others. Discretion, and agreement of boundaries on what can be passed on to whom, is another hallmark of the accomplished networker.

Perspective

One of the key characteristics of resilient people is that they have a good sense of perspective. They don't overreact to setbacks or treat a slight as a mortal insult. Instead, they keep a sense of proportion, attaching due weight to unwelcome developments, always eager to start planning a response rather than railing against the unfairness of what has happened.

Not everyone is naturally blessed with a sense of perspective. Many of us dwell on problems for longer than they really warrant; we need others to help us get things into some kind of balance. Unfortunately, the people who often have the most difficulty with this are often also those most reluctant to turn to others for advice. A similar problem can arise when someone understands *intellectually* that the situation they're in isn't life-threatening, but the way they feel stubbornly refuses to change to reflect this understanding. Of course, input from others can help here too – not perhaps by instantly transforming what the sufferer is feeling, but by accelerating the process which allows them to get the issue into perspective, and then move on.

Reassurance

At times, you may feel that you really need someone on your side; someone who will reassure you that you are on the right track, that you are not to blame, that your thinking is sound, or whatever it takes to help you move into a more positive frame of mind. This can help you build your confidence levels, eliminate any paranoid tendencies and reduce feelings of isolation. In our research, most participants said that reassurance from others really helped them build their resilience.

> 'I do talk issues through with friends to get some perspective. They help me to see that I'm not the only person facing the problem, and there may be different approaches I could try.'

Feedback

As well as offering reassurance, other people can also provide feedback. This means sharing your situation, your thoughts and ideas with another individual in order to get their objective, dispassionate response. This individual needs to be someone whose judgement and experience you respect. They must also be prepared to challenge you. Without this, there is a risk that they will merely agree with everything you say, which could well be comforting, but which serves no real purpose when it comes to testing out your thinking. 'Yes men' may be welcome in the courts of the 'great men' whose delusions of grandeur helped bring the global financial system to its knees in 2008, but they add no value to the development of sane and sound thinking.

Learning

For some people, having the opportunity to talk things through with a mentor or coach, and benefit from the wisdom of their experience, is very helpful. Such people will help you to focus on any lessons you can glean from your experience, and put corrective action plans in place. They can help build your resilience.

'I'm pretty self-reliant. I rarely talk to friends or family about work issues. I like to use advisors and mentors, trying things out on them that are bothering me.'

Opportunity

'Opportunity networks' are a mainstay of business success. Research suggests that as many as 50% of people say they found their current job through friends and family. Very few senior positions are filled by responding to advertisements. Most go to existing contacts, some of which may have been made relatively recently. These days, with the advent of 'relationship marketing', new business leads come less through cold calling and more through word-of-mouth recommendation and personal relationships. It really is *who* you know (as much as *what* you know) that makes a difference.

Opportunity networks involve establishing clearly what you want for the future – short, medium and long term – and identifying people who will be able to help you achieve your aims. More about this in Chapter 11.

HOW TO NETWORK

As already mentioned, some people are natural networkers; they have no difficulty forging strong relationships with a range of people, expressing their needs and 'naming' their emotions (ie actually pinpointing how they are feeling – happy, relieved, hopeful etc – rather than just saying 'I'm fine'). However, for those who are not naturals, the following guidelines may help:

- Be clear about what you want to achieve
- Act well in advance
- Reframe your thinking
- Ensure any networking is a two-way process

- Have an adult to adult conversation
- Be interested in the other person
- Ask for advice

We will now expand on each of these points to help you improve your networking skills.

Be clear about what you want to achieve

First of all, you need to have a clear idea of what it is you want to achieve. Do you want to pick someone's brains about a particular issue, or is it more about discussing mutual opportunities? Are you just interested in what another person is doing? If so, to what end? Knowing what you want to achieve will help point you in the direction of the most appropriate people.

Act well in advance

Nine times out of 10, it helps to start building relationships well before you actually need them. The development of mutual trust, respect, interest – even friendship – takes time. And even if it's a small favour or piece of advice you're after, people won't thank you for putting pressure on them at the last minute. Stephen Covey, author of *The 7 Habits of Highly Effective People*, developed the idea of the 'emotional bank account'. Like any other account, the balance starts at zero. As time goes on, we deposit emotional units into the account as we invest in relationships and build trust. When we do this, the relationship grows. Similarly, we can make withdrawals; but when we do so, it is important to apologize, and to make sure that the overall balance remains as high as possible.

During the financial crisis that hit in the late Noughties, emails started flying around from those recently made redundant, keen to rekindle relationships and seek out opportunities.

Those fortunate enough still to be in work didn't have the time to oblige everyone who asked to talk to them. They had to be selective. Generally speaking, they chose people who had helped them in the past, or who had at least sustained the relationship. But those who had neglected them, or had made too many withdrawals from the emotional bank account, often found themselves receiving a dose of their own medicine.

Reframe your thinking

Some people feel bad about asking others for favours, even when their request is perfectly reasonable – the student seeking an extension on his essay after the laptop containing his notes is stolen, or the teacher asking his principal for a few days' leave to sort out domestic arrangements while his partner is in hospital. Some people even feel bad asking others for their time, to talk through a problem they are having at work for example. They go into the conversation thinking, 'This person will just think I'm wasting their time, they won't be interested in my experience'. As a result, they may well come across as self-deprecating – so their anxiety about time-wasting becomes a self-fulfilling prophesy.

To minimize this risk, you need to be in the right mindset. Instead of thinking, 'I might be wasting [an individual's] time', turn this around to something more constructive and positive. You will get a far better result if you think, 'How can I make this a valuable experience for the other person?' Similarly, a mindset of, 'They're not going to be interested in what I have to say' is unlikely to be productive. If instead you think, 'They *will* be interested in what I have to say', it might be true, or it might be false, but it's more likely to be true if you believe it. And, if you have a problem you need to talk through, instead of worrying that you're being a nuisance, you might think about the benefits to the other person of being alerted to the issue – or even, 'I have every right to flag this up; it's getting in the way of my performance'.

Ensure any networking is a two-way process

Clearly, the mindset described in the previous section will help ensure that networking is a two-way process. Instead of thinking that you are thrusting yourself upon the other person, being a burden to them, you need to believe that the conversation will be of interest to the other person too – that they are going to be engaged with you, and might even get something out of it for themselves. To help with this, it's useful to think through in advance what actually might be useful for them, no matter how small. What can you give in return? Even if you can't give them something right away, you may be able to do so in the future, and can mention this possibility.

Have an adult-to-adult conversation

Again, your frame of mind will affect the impact you have. All too often, people come across as being subservient or significantly more junior when they're asking others for favours. In 'Transactional Analysis' terms, they become childlike, while the other person assumes the parent role – for example, being patronizing, issuing orders or assuming seniority. This demands obedience and the parent–child conversation is perpetuated. Successful networking almost always stems from adult to adult conversations, where equality is a given. The same weight is attached to the opinions of both parties, with neither assuming superiority or a 'right to be right', despite the fact that one person may be asking another for a favour, or even for the other to become their mentor or advisor.

Be interested in the other person

Another trap that many people fall into is to become so focused on themselves — how they're coming across, whether they're being articulate, how they can ask the questions they want to ask etc — that they forget to be interested in the other person. It is important that you show interest in the person you are speaking to. One way of doing this is by asking intelligent, informed questions. This will not only provide you with valuable information — which could lead to opportunity — but will also convey a more confident impression.

Ask for advice

Research clearly indicates that people are most likely to agree to a meeting if they are asked to give advice. It is always flattering to be asked for guidance, and also non-threatening. People tend to be less guarded and suspicious if you say you'd just like to pick their brains.

MAINTAINING YOUR NETWORK

Your network will develop and mature over time. Some people will drop out, others will take their place. As the years pass, the number, range and depth of your relationships with others will grow. But your database of contacts is like a garden; without ongoing care and attention, the whole thing becomes tangled and unwieldy. The only thing you can do with it if it reaches this stage is prune heavily and pretty much start again.

So, you need to manage and maintain your network — actively. This means finding a way of being in regular contact with people, and *regular* means *appropriate*! For some people, a Christmas card or occasional email will be enough. With others, you may need to phone them monthly to demonstrate your support and interest. Listen carefully to what they have to say, and make a note of any developments in their lives. It may be possible to invite them to events – business or otherwise. But you need to be selective.

Pareto's law dictates that 80% of any benefit will come from 20% of your contacts. On this basis, there is probably only a small group of people you absolutely need to stay in touch with. Work out who these people are and develop a strategy for maintaining your relationship with them. Be careful not to misjudge this; there's nothing worse than becoming a pain in the neck to someone. As the best form of business relationship operates on an emotional bank account basis, establish what your contact is getting out of it, as well as what you are. Think laterally, there may be all sorts of things that you – or other members of your network – can offer them. Finally, update and review your network regularly. Are there any gaps? Are you being sufficiently forward-thinking? Could you usefully introduce some members of your network to others?

STRIKING A BALANCE

At the start of this chapter, we noted that individual account-ability is a key characteristic of resilience – and it is. However, this needs to be balanced with seeking support and input from others. The view that asking for help is a sign of weakness is out-dated – and inaccurate. Involving others will help to enhance, not diminish, your resilience. Sociability is inborn; the only surprise is that so many of us find it difficult. The skills and tech-niques discussed in this chapter should feel neither awkward nor Machiavellian; to excel at them, you need only rediscover an innate, childhood ability.

Chapter 10

I beg to differ – managing conflict

A fight, a row, a ruckus, a rift, or at the least a serious disagreement – that's how most people view conflict. But conflict is broader than that. One widely used definition is 'any situation in which your agenda, desires or views differ from that of another person'. On the basis of this definition, it's clear that conflict is all around us, every day. Small wonder, then, that being willing to face up to conflict, rather than avoid it, is another key characteristic of highly resilient people. And yet, the very thought of conflict can turn many people into quivering wrecks. People fear conflict; they avoid it or bottle it up and allow it to fester, sometimes for years. Regardless of whether you choose to confront an issue or not, conflict is one of the most frequent causes of stress and anxiety.

PERSONALITY DIFFERENCES

Interestingly, what constitutes conflict for one person might just be seen as healthy competition or stimulating debate by another – tolerance and 'enjoyment' levels vary enormously between individuals. Personality also has a significant bearing. Take three individuals. One is highly rational, liking to analyze situations thoroughly and review all the data before making a decision.

We'll call this person the 'rational'. Another is sensitive, a real 'people person', only happy when everyone else is, and always willing to help others sort out their problems. This individual is the 'emotional'. The third is driven, ambitious and impatient, highly focused on achieving their goal – and being seen to do so. We'll call this person the 'competitive'. What constitutes conflict for each of these types?

The 'rational' is only too happy to have an intellectual argument, at as detailed a level as possible. For this person, this is not conflict, it is healthy debate. However, the 'emotional' would not see it that way, probably taking some of the comments personally. To the 'competitive', it would feel like the 'rational' is getting in the way of progress, putting up obstacles. Again, this is a conflict situation.

As well as having different views about what conflict is, the three individuals identified above also differ hugely in terms of how they solve problems. The 'emotional' may, in the first instance, try to avoid having the conversation, on the basis that they don't want to hurt anyone's feelings. However, if they do choose to confront the issue, they are likely to want to probe feelings and reasons for behaviour – to get beneath the surface. Failure for the 'emotional' would be both parties walking away unhappy.

It's a very different story for the 'rational'. They will want to be direct and factual – emotions don't really come into it at all. Failure for them would be if the 'right' decision is not taken.

More straightforwardly, for the 'competitive', failure would simply be them not 'winning' the argument, not getting their way.

Conflicting personalities

Two people had to work closely together. One was an engineer, the other an ex-banker. They were two of the most powerful people in a global organization, but they never saw eye to eye because their personalities and approaches were so different from one another's. The engineer would take a problem and walk away with it. He wouldn't speak to another soul about the matter until he had personally analyzed the situation and arrived at the solution - sharing ideas at an early stage and sounding people out didn't work for him at all. This type of thinking is called 'analytic'. The ex-banker, on the other hand, was more of a 'synthetic' thinker. He liked to brainstorm ideas and 'fly kites'. He thought it essential to seek the input and ideas of all stakeholders, and to do so at an early stage in the thinking process.

The two individuals circled round each other, often talking at cross purposes and consistently misinterpreting each other's motives. People dreaded their being in the same room together; their relationship was hugely disruptive to the organization.

Despite mediation, the conflict was never resolved. Eventually one of the individuals left.

WHY IS CONFLICT DIFFICULT?

Many people say that conflict is healthy – and it can be, particularly when a group of people are trying to be creative: without disagreement and challenge you don't really generate new ideas. Conflict can stimulate change.

However, conflict can also be disruptive and disturbing. In 1995, James Wall and Ronda Callister, management specialists at the University of Missouri, reported the results of a study which found no empirical support for the idea that conflict is merely 'healthy competition' (although that's the way many people choose to view it when they don't want to be involved in confrontation). What's more, contrary to prevailing beliefs, Wall and Callister suggested that conflict avoided is better than conflict well-managed. In their view, people feel more positive about one another if there have been no issues between them than if there have been issues and they've managed to sort things out. This might be because there is always some residual ill-feeling – a memory of the behaviours and slights that caused the disagreement in the first place. Perhaps this is one of the reasons why people are nervous about conflict. But there are plenty more. Cast your eye down the list below. In a conflict situation, how many of these might cross your mind?

- This person doesn't like me
- This person doesn't rate me
- I might be wrong
- I'm not so sure of my facts
- I could be exposed
- I could hurt the other person's feelings
- It will take too much time to sort things out
- It's not a big deal really
- I don't want to rock the boat
- If I criticize them they might criticize me in the future
- I feel really uncomfortable about this
- There's no point even talking about this, it'll make no difference
- I can't be bothered

Of course, not everyone finds conflict difficult. Some people actually relish it (certain politicians come to mind), actively seeking out every opportunity for disagreement and debate. We'll come back to this shortly, but first we need to take a look at why the ability to deal effectively with conflict is associated with high resilience.

Ongoing, unresolved conflict makes you feel bad, and can seriously impede your progress. Such conflict may endure because you don't like disharmony, or can't bear others disagreeing with you. Whatever your personal reaction to conflict, failing to manage it can pull you seriously out of shape. It may keep you awake, stress you out and (in extreme cases) provoke physical and psychological problems. Take the manager we worked with recently – healthy, happy and phenomenally successful in life – whose boss didn't share his view of what his next role should be. There was no acrimony, the relationship was perfectly friendly, but it affected the individual so profoundly that he went into therapy.

Resilient people manage conflict. They are alert to the potential for problems. They have the strength of character not to take criticism and differences of opinion personally (unless, of course, the comments *are* intended to be personal). They also have the wisdom to know what needs to be done (do they need to confront the conflict or let things lie for a while?), and possess the courage, open-mindedness and interpersonal skills to handle disagreement. To be resilient, you have to be able to deal with conflict, and to do so effectively.

In our research, we found that almost all members of the R-team prefer to deal with issues early; they certainly don't avoid conflict. They try to view any problem from all angles – they seek feedback from people, remain receptive to other people's ideas and thoughts, and bide their time until the situation is ripe for resolution.

> '**Sometimes it's better to deal with conflict on the spot, sometimes it's better to deal with it a bit later, and sometimes not at all. The important thing is to feel that you are bigger than the issue, that you are in control of when and how (or if at all) to resolve it.**'

'Over the years I've learnt to do three things with conflict. First, when I see conflict looming, I take time to think the issue through, sometimes sleeping on it. Then I try to get into the other person's shoes to understand where they're coming from and how I can make my pitch more palatable. Finally, I try to leave the other person some "wriggle room" - a way to save face.'

The results of the NMRQ support this finding; those who answer 'agree' in response to the question 'I tend to avoid conflict' emerge as being less resilient.

There also seems to be a link between a tendency to avoid conflict and a more generalized failure to act. People who avoid conflict also procrastinate, suffer from 'analysis paralysis' (an inability to act or make a decision due to excessive data-gathering, research etc) and admit to indecisiveness. Interestingly, these less resilient people also say that others often describe them as being laid back, suggesting that if you are seen in this way you are more likely to be tolerant, to roll with the punches and accept what, to others, might be *un*acceptable. Highly resilient people, by contrast, are more likely to take action.

HOW TO MANAGE CONFLICT

Kenneth W Thomas and Ralph H Kilmann are leading authorities on conflict. They maintain that, in a conflict situation, you have a couple of basic decisions to make – how assertive to be, and how cooperative to be. In their terminology, 'assertiveness' relates to the extent to which you want to 'win' the argument, or for your view to prevail. Cooperativeness is just the opposite – how happy you are for the other party to get what they want.

Choose a style

According to Thomas and Kilmann, depending on the decisions you make about how assertive or cooperative to be, you have five basic styles of conflict resolution to choose from. These are shown in the diagram below.

Conflict resolution styles

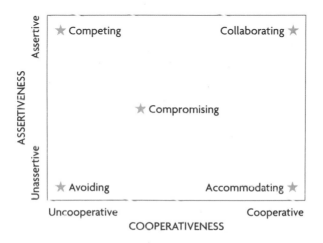

1 Competing

> 'Most disagreements are about one of three things –
> where we are starting from, where we want to get to,
> and how to get there. I never try to hide the fact that I
> don't agree with someone. Instead I express my opinion
> early, ask the other person how they think we can resolve
> our differences, and then ask other people for their
> views – usually in the hope that they'll support mine!'

Competing is highly assertive, but not at all cooperative. It is the style you would use when you want to win; for example, it might be appropriate in a situation where you know you're right (or at least strongly believe that you're right), or for issues that you feel passionately about. You would also want to compete if the matter was a legal requirement or a moral dilemma. Someone using this style could come across as being authoritative and directive, even dictatorial. On the other hand, it might be that this person is so charismatic and influential – really selling the benefits of their position – that, although technically they've 'won', the other person still walks away feeling good. Depending on how you choose to use this style, there is a risk that it can cause bad feeling and damage relationships, especially if you are the kind of person who competes frequently.

2 Collaborating

> **'My attitude to conflict has changed over time.
> When I was young, I was very argumentative
> and ready for a verbal fight; very provocative.
> Now I try and go for the "win-win".'**

Collaborating is both highly assertive and highly cooperative – the archetypal win-win style. This approach is suitable when the matter is important enough to warrant investing in the best possible outcome, and one which satisfies the key requirements of both parties. It may well be that, if the first person walks into the conflict wanting 'Solution A', and the second person wants 'Solution B', having talked it all through they together come up with 'Solution C', which they are both happy with. Collaborating is a constructive approach to conflict. Too much of it, however, can be overly time-consuming and wearing for others.

3 Compromising

> **'I move quickly into compromise mode, always willing to
> put myself in the middle - say, between the marketing
> people (who usually want us to lend people money) and
> the credit people (who usually don't). My approach is to
> listen to both sides, then replay the story as I understand
> it, demanding that those involved tell me where I've got
> it wrong. Once the parties hear the whole story, and stop
> representing their silos, conflict tends to fade away.'**

Compromising is the middle ground. It's when you choose to strike a deal – a classic negotiation. You get some of what you want, and so too does the other person. More rapid than collaborating, compromising is a pragmatic approach, and therefore appropriate for less important matters. There is a risk, however, that neither party walks away feeling quite satisfied.

4 Avoiding

> 'While I would normally deal with conflict, I've
> realized that some battles just aren't worth fighting.
> I'm talking about issues which are unimportant
> in the grand scheme of things, or problems
> that will sort themselves out over time.'

Avoiding is neither assertive nor cooperative. Although unresolved conflict can be very toxic, an avoiding strategy can be appropriate in certain situations – when the matter is totally trivial, for example, or when it's likely to resolve itself. You might also wish to adopt an avoiding strategy when it would be more appropriate for someone else to deal with the issue. On occasion, while an avoiding strategy might not be the best approach, it might be the only option available – there are situations when a resolution is so unlikely that there's no point even trying; some battles are just not worth fighting.

5 Accommodating

> 'Some mountains can't be moved. It's important not
> to waste energy on things you cannot affect.'

Accommodating is the exact opposite of competing – highly cooperative, but not assertive. It is the style you would use when the relationship with the other party is more important than the matter in hand. Accommodating is the approach you would adopt when you are happy for the other person to get their way – maybe the issue isn't important to you, or just a lot less important to you than it is to them. Alternatively, as you start to discuss the matter, you might realize that they have a point, that their idea would actually work better than yours.

Thinking back to Stephen Covey's emotional bank account (see page 131), accommodating is the approach you would adopt when making a 'deposit'. Again, there is a risk involved – if you overuse this style, you might be seen as a pushover. Others might then start to take advantage of you. Still, even when you do accommodate, things do not always work out as planned. Sometimes the other party will simply not play ball, in which case, you must move on.

Negative fall-out

Someone very used to dealing with conflict in his professional life found that he had a difficult situation to deal with at home. Happily married, and with two lovely children, he found to his horror that he was falling out of favour with his father-in-law. This came to a head when the father-in-law wrote a letter to his daughter criticizing the husband, on all sorts of issues, including how he treated her and the children. The couple decided that the allegations were totally unfounded - in fact, they were shocked because they genuinely couldn't recognize any of what the old man was saying - and responded to this effect.

The situation worsened over time. The criticisms became stronger, and the father even claimed that others in the family found the husband hard to get on with. He later admitted that this was a lie, but he did not retract any of the other allegations he had made. After a prolonged period, the father-in-law wrote to his daughter declaring that he would not be seeing her, the husband or their children again. He said that, although he loved his daughter, he didn't like what she had become. Nor did he like his son-in-law. The man was prepared to lose his daughter and contact with his grandchildren for perceived slights and misdemeanors which were unrecognizable to those apparently responsible.

The couple accepted that the conflict had gone too far to attempt reconciliation, and that the only course of action now available to them was enforced 'accommodation'; they had absolutely no choice in the matter. Had the father-in-law seen sense, the ideal approach in this situation would have been collaboration, but he was just not open to it.

According to Thomas and Kilmann, all these styles are appropriate, at different times and in different circumstances. The trick is to know which to use, and having the skills to pull it off. In choosing your conflict resolution style, you have to consider the personality of the other person as well as the nature of the conflict. The trouble is, most people tend to use only a couple of styles, driven by their personality. For example, some might tend to inhabit the bottom half of the matrix – they are not very good at asserting their own requirements. This may be because they don't like to ask other people for favours, especially for themselves. Or they may just prefer it when other people get what they want. Contrast this individual with someone who habitually competes, occasionally collaborating when they believe their proposed solution could also incorporate the other person's wishes. This person is highly assertive; they are only cooperative when it won't diminish their own chance of winning.

Of course, there are many possible combinations of styles, creating a diverse range of different individual profiles, some of which may appear to be contradictory. For example, it is quite common for someone to be highly competitive *and* highly avoidant. On the face of it, these strategies seem to be diametrically opposed; however, when you talk to people who fit this profile they are unsurprised, saying that – when a conflict arises – they quickly consider a) whether they can win, and b) whether they think it's worth the trouble. On the basis of the answers to these questions, they decide whether to compete or avoid.

To establish your own preferences, you can take the 'Thomas Kilmann Conflict Mode Instrument' (TKI) and access further information at **www.opp.eu.com/psychometric_instruments/ tki**. However, if you just want a feel for your personal preferences – a snapshot – study the comments below. Which most accurately reflect your preferred approach to conflict?

Approaches to conflict

Competing	**Collaborating**
My way or the highway!	Two heads are better than one
It's vitally important to win	Let's really explore the issues
I know I'm right about this	I try to use a problem-
I'm usually firm in pursuing my goals	solving approach
I'm good at selling the merits and	It's useful to seek the
benefits of my approach to others	help and input of others
	in conflict situations
	Let's get all the issues
	into the open

Compromising
Let's strike a deal
Can we split the difference?
Let's find the middle ground
I am happy to concede on some points if you do too
It's important to be pragmatic about this

Avoiding	**Accommodating**
I'll think about it tomorrow	It would be my pleasure
I hate confrontation	It's obviously very important to you
It's not such a big deal	I often pander to other
I don't want to make a	people's wishes
fuss about this	I try not to hurt the other
There's no point even	person's feelings
raising the issue	It's often more important to
	preserve the relationship
	than win the argument

Interpreting your score

If you mentally tick more statements in one section than in another, you are more likely to adopt that style of conflict resolution. As mentioned earlier, all five approaches are appropriate at times, but you need to understand when those times might be. Nine times out of 10, a naturally avoidant person can persuade themselves that 'best left unsaid' is the right strategy, whereas someone who is highly competitive will feel very strongly, in most situations, that they are right, and should therefore fight.

It is really important to be honest with yourself and challenge your natural tendencies if you are to handle conflict situations well. Rigorously analyzing each situation, and sticking with the strategy that the analysis produces, will help you to get it right. When approaching a conflict situation, try asking yourself the following questions:

- What has caused the conflict?
- What is the history, ie who's done what so far?
- What is the nature of the conflict – for example, personality clashes, unacceptable behaviour, differences in approach, political problems, incompatible structures and cultures, breakdown in processes etc?
- Who are the parties involved?
- What are their personalities?
- What do they want, ideally, as an outcome?
- What do you want, ideally, as an outcome?
- What, therefore, is the best approach?

Going through this list of questions will help you to understand the nature of the conflict, and decide what the best approach might be. Of course, you still need the strength of character to pull it off — whether that involves biting your tongue on this occasion, or confronting the individual involved head on — but you will be clear about what you should be doing to reach resolution.

Most people feel glad once they've tackled an issue, and often say that it wasn't as bad as they thought it was going to be. Members of the R-team are very alert to the dangers of 'ducking out' — of dodging the ball — but phlegmatic about occasionally having to admit defeat.

> **'People who aren't resilient try to avoid conflict because they are fearful - of losing, or of making the other person angry. But if you don't confront, you effectively concede the argument; you then have no right to be resentful when your view doesn't prevail.'**

Involve others

Sometimes you need to involve a third party in resolving a conflict — a mediator. This is a conflict-handling tactic in its own right, with a success rate estimated at 60%, according to Wall and Callister. However, this figure may be artificially low because interventions frequently attack the causes of conflict (rather than picking off the symptoms), and so can actually prevent future problems. Intervention has been found to strengthen interpersonal relationships and reduce stress; it is an extremely useful weapon in the armoury of the highly resilient individual. What is more, Wall and Callister calculate that 75% of disputants are satisfied with the results of intervention, which leads to a 77% compliance rate.

Conflict has the ability to pull many of us seriously out of shape, and often for long periods of time. The ability to recognize conflict, to understand it and deal with it in a way which, wherever possible, causes minimum stress and leaves the relationship intact, is a vital component of the resilience toolkit.

Having explored (in Part 1) what resilience is, and where it comes from, in Part 2 we focused on how resilient people deal with the challenges that life presents – and how their thinking and behaviour distinguishes them from those of us who are not so resilient. Now, in Part 3, we explain how you can develop your own resilience, starting with an opportunity to assess your personal RQ.

Part ③

Becoming more resilient

Chapter 11

Raising the bar

Throughout this book, we have shown how some people are more resilient than others, and that the threshold at which resilience comes into play differs from person to person – we each have a different reaction to stress, adversity and crisis.

As far back as Chapter 1, we noted that is would be useful if we could measure our response to crisis, identify our personal tipping point, in some way. Similarly, it would be useful if we could rate personal and organizational crises on an objective metric – the psychological equivalent of the Richter scale, which allows meteorologists to 'measure' earthquakes. Useful, but impossible, because beyond numbers and statistics, crisis cannot be calibrated nor, indeed, can our response to it. Context combines with subjective factors, arising from individual differences in personality and experience, to make a mockery of the very idea. Whatever its nature or cause, individual responses to crisis vary. For example, the 2008 credit crunch hit some more than others, and not just in their pocket. Those who had seen it coming could take the 'shock' better, and respond faster; as mentioned previously, the ability to anticipate stressful events helps build resilience.

Since crisis cannot be callibrated, you need to be aware of your own personal 'pain threshold'. Up to a point, challenge and change are energizing, but beyond this they trigger stress, anxiety and incompetence.

To build resilience, you must understand your own threshold – how much pressure you can take, what type of challenge is likely to increase your stress to an uncomfortable level, and what the warning signs are. You can then take steps to raise your threshold. Having said that, no matter how high you manage to set the bar, there will always be times when it is exceeded. The trick then is to be able to bounce back, better and stronger than before.

WHAT IS YOUR PERSONAL RESILIENCE QUOTIENT (RQ)?

We have already discussed in some depth what it takes to bounce back from tough times and, in many cases, have given you questionnaires and checklists to help you assess where you sit on the various fronts, for example, how optimistic you are, how susceptible to stress etc.

Here, however, we now provide a short questionnaire (questions are taken from the NMRQ) covering the strongest indicators of resilience, to allow you to get a feel for your overall level of resilience – your personal Resilience Quotient (RQ). For each question, award yourself a score of 1 to 5, where 1 = I strongly disagree and 5 = I strongly agree. Then calculate your total score. It is important that you are honest, essential that you don't kid yourself. Understanding the specific areas in which you need to improve will enable you to get the most out of the 10-point plan that follows.

Resilience Quotient questionnaire

Question	Score
1 In a difficult situation, my thoughts immediately turn to what can be done to put things right	
2 I influence what I can rather than worrying about what I can't	
3 I don't take criticism personally	
4 I generally manage to keep things in perspective	
5 I am calm in a crisis	
6 I am good at finding solutions to new problems	
7 I wouldn't describe myself as an anxious person	
8 I don't tend to avoid conflict	
9 I try to control events rather than being a victim of my circumstances	
10 I trust my intuition	
11 I manage my stress levels well	
12 I feel confident and secure in my position	
Total score	

Interpreting your score

So what does your score mean?

0–37 (a **developing** level of resilience)
Your score indicates that, while you may not always feel at the mercy of events, you would benefit from developing aspects of your behaviour which would increase your personal resilience. This might include changing your response to setbacks.

38–43 (an **established** level of resilience)
Your score indicates that, although you may occasionally have tough days when you can't make things go your way, you rarely feel ready to give up. About a third of our development sample

fall into this category. You may need to develop more of a sense of perspective on setbacks.

44–48 (a **strong** level of resilience)
Your above average score indicates that you're pretty good at rolling with the punches (whoever is throwing them!), and that you have an impressive track record of turning threats into opportunities. You seem to have a healthy sense of perspective.

49+ (an **exceptional** level of resilience)
This score indicates that you are very resilient most of the time, and rarely fail to bounce back – whatever life throws at you. You believe that you are unusually adept at 'making your own luck', though you may need to check from time to time that others appreciate your robust approach, particularly those who aspire to match your resilience.

While your overall score is of course a useful indication of your overall level of resilience, it is also important for you to review your responses to individual questions.

Look back at the questionnaire; on which questions did you score high? On which did you score low? You might also want to go into more depth and understand the specific areas in which you scored high, average and low. You can do this by logging on to **www.testyourrq.com** where you will find further information about the NMRQ and the full online questionnaire.

Once you have focused your attention on your own development requirements, you can start working on making the change, using the 10-point plan described opposite.

HOW TO INCREASE YOUR RESILIENCE

Regardless of your current RQ, the following 10 steps will help you to boost your resilience levels. For those of you who fall into the 'developing' category, it would probably be of benefit to work through all 10 steps. For others, however, there may well be one or two areas you need to focus on, in which case you can go straight to the relevant sections.

10-point resilience plan

1 Visualize success

2 Boost your self-esteem

3 Enhance your self-efficacy; take control

4 Become more optimistic

5 Manage your stress

6 Improve your decision-making

7 Ask for help

8 Deal with conflict

9 Learn

10 Be yourself

1 Visualize success

A key characteristic of resilient people is that they create their own vision of success. Merely being in possession of this vision helps them achieve their goals because it provides a clear sense of where they're headed, and enables them subconsciously to work towards it; their 'inner programmes' take over. It is vital, therefore, to create a vision of the future – and to make it as rounded and vibrant as you possibly can. And it must be based on what is currently possible – resilient people don't waste time on impossible dreams or hankering after things they'll clearly never have. Resilient people recognize that there is a fine line between goals or ambitions being stretching and being unrealistic; what's more, they know where to draw this line.

In a world where expectations and situations are constantly changing, part of the bouncing back process might involve reframing your definition of success and shifting your parameters. Where necessary, you may need to redefine yourself in terms of:

- Whom you benchmark yourself against – your COMPARATORS
- How you view your own capability and performance – your COMPETENCE
- What constitutes wealth and a fair wage for what you do – your COMPENSATION
- The way you come across to others – your CREDIBILITY

Each of these concepts is explained below.

Comparators

Everyone compares themselves with others; it's natural. It's also natural to look at people who have a little bit more than you do, and aspire to that level. When circumstances change, however, your comparators tend not to; you continue to look to the same benchmark group for affirmation. The Joneses may be long gone, but you still want to keep up with them! Of course, some people have a more magnanimous outlook, finding it easy to feel grateful for what they have while accepting that their relative good fortune brings with it a responsibility to help others less fortunate. Such an outlook offers some psychological benefits to the natural altruist, allowing them to be positive about what they have rather than negative about what they don't have. Unfortunately, this is not the easiest mindset to acquire if you start from a more selfish, materialistic set of values.

In tough times, it is essential that you take a step back and review your comparators, adopting a more appropriate and realistic benchmark group, endeavouring to count your blessings rather than curse your losses.

Competence

In a world of deadlines, targets and instant messaging, it can be difficult to find time to develop yourself outside work. So, there is a significant risk that you 'are what you do'. If you find yourself in a situation where this sense of identity is taken away from you – you've been moved into a different type of role at work, feel as though you've been demoted or, indeed, you've lost your job – this can have a significant impact on how you see yourself. In this situation, it is important to remember that it's often not your competence that has changed but simply your circumstances. Again, you may need to adjust your parameters, helping you to view change positively and to recognize the value of your contribution.

If you are made redundant, Professor Cary Cooper advises that the most important thing you can do is to stay busy. This might mean learning a new skill, furthering your education or doing some voluntary work. Whatever it is, the sense of being active and contributing will help to maintain your confidence levels, which will ultimately ease your passage back into paid work again – if this is what you want to do.

Compensation

The 2008 credit crunch affected all levels of society, to a greater or lesser degree. Only a minority managed to protect their absolute position, whether in terms of salary, fees, perks, pension pot or investment income. The crunch reminded us that house prices and salaries do not always go up, and that businesses (from Woolworths to Lehman Brothers) do sometimes go down. It also reminded us of the need to cut our coat according to our cloth. When salaries are frozen and savings offer little return, money worries can encroach, especially if you are overextending yourself. When finances are tight, it is essential that you reappraise your budget, understand what is realistic – and then effect any necessary changes in your spending. Having a grip on your expenses will help you to survive financially, and ensure resilience. If you fail to do this, there is a risk that your debt will spiral out of control – and you with it.

Credibility

So, you've defined your vision; now you need to sell it to others. It's frequently other people who stop you from changing; paradoxically, the reason why they refuse to accept the 'new, improved' version of yourself is often because *you* haven't entirely bought in to it. Every sales person knows that the first step to a successful sale is selling the idea to yourself. Until you've done this, you have little chance of coming across as credible. Putting a positive spin on what you're doing in your own mind will help you to feel better about yourself which – in turn – will be conveyed in what you say to others. Your own positive view of self, coupled with the endorsement of others, will build self-esteem and enhance your sense of success.

2 Boost your self-esteem

As mentioned in Chapter 3, self-esteem is essential if you are going to demonstrate high levels of resilience. Some people are naturally blessed with high self-esteem. Others need to work on it – which means you need to know where it comes from. As also mentioned in Chapter 3, there are many sources of self-esteem. What are yours? Write down what makes you feel good about yourself. Then review your list. Is it too narrow? Are you one of those people who rely almost entirely on success at work to boost your self-esteem, or maybe your abilities as a home-maker? Or are you perhaps highly competitive – it doesn't matter about the nature of the activity, just as long as you're 'winning' you feel good about yourself?

The danger of having a single source of self-esteem – or even just a couple – is that if one dries up (for example, you're made redundant, or you lose your house and children through divorce), you will find it difficult to maintain your levels of self-esteem, which will then affect your ability to recover. So, you should 'build out' the list of things that make you feel good about yourself, making it as broad and robust as you can. It is important that you believe in the value of this list, and that you acknowledge every time you engage with one of your sources, giving yourself the credit for it.

Many people take their strengths for granted, and so tend to underestimate their own abilities. As a result, they don't even know what should go on the list in the first place. When complimented, a surprisingly high proportion of people respond by saying, 'It was nothing really – anyone could do it'. In this instance, self-deprecation can be counterproductive. It is essential that you establish what you're good at, what you like about yourself, what other people value about you, and the contribution you make – at work, home and to wider society.

Sometimes it takes someone else holding up the mirror to help you appreciate what your strengths are.

In an ideal world, your self-esteem would be generated from within. In this way, you are not dependent on others. However, as long as you are developing your own self-esteem, it doesn't hurt to factor in external sources too.

It is important to heed and value any praise you receive – to listen to it and take it on board. It is interesting to note that, in formal appraisal situations, many people barely acknowledge the positive feedback they receive as they are so focused on the negative. If you ask them what the feedback was, they'll probably be able to tell you all the things they need to do differently, but struggle to recall specifics about the positives.

As well as listening to feedback in a formal setting, you can also actively seek the views of others. Asking people how they think you performed in certain situations often elicits some very useful information. You can use the positive feedback to help boost your confidence, while any negatives must be viewed as an opportunity for improvement. And once you act on this feedback – and address any shortcomings – you must give yourself credit for having done so, further enhancing your levels of self-esteem.

And what about your relationships? Think of the people who love you, like you, respect you, enjoy your company and appreciate what you do for them. Why do they feel this way about you? It's because you are clearly a valued partner, friend, relative, colleague or confidant to them. Use this knowledge to fuel your self-esteem yet further.

Checklist

✓ What are the things that you're good at, the things that you can feel positive about? Write them down

✓ Remind yourself of this list from time to time

✓ Recognize what other people appreciate and value about you

✓ Allow people to praise you, and resist the temptation to brush positive feedback aside

✓ When something goes wrong, avoid beating yourself up. Instead, focus your energy on what can be done to rectify the situation

✓ Try not to compare yourself with other people

✓ When things go well for others, feel genuinely pleased for them

✓ Enjoy it when something goes better than you thought it would

✓ Silently praise yourself

3 Enhance your self-efficacy; take control

Self-efficacy is another key characteristic of resilient people. In order to demonstrate your self-efficacy, you have to take control of situations, thoughts and emotions. This ability is a core attribute of resilient people.

As mentioned in Chapter 5, reframing is a useful technique to help you get into the right frame of mind to take control. Interestingly, our experience has shown that there are a number of unhelpful, commonly held beliefs – 'drag anchors' – that need to be dispelled if you are to build your resilience. Here are six of the most common.

1 I am the victim of my personal history

Of course, your past has had an impact on your present, but too many people become victims of their circumstances, finding excuses not to act, not to change, because of their personal history. They therefore spend valuable time and energy explaining why things *can't* be done, rather than focusing on how they *could* be done.

Although personal change is difficult, it is not impossible. When you think about it, you are probably surrounded by people who have successfully achieved a shift in their behaviour. The recovering alcoholic who has managed to give up drinking, the habitual worrier who has become much less anxious in recent years, or the autocratic boss who's started to seek input from others and has adopted a far more inclusive approach. For the alcoholic, this may well have involved some intensive therapy, so too perhaps the worrier. The autocratic boss might have benefited from training, or the services of an executive coach. Whatever the cause of the change, there is no need (within reason) for you to allow personal history to limit your potential. To quote Stephen Covey again: 'Live out of your imagination, not your history.'

2 There's so much to do, it's not even worth trying

Many people complain that their lives are increasingly complex, and that they are having to do more with less. It's not surprising, then, that many fall into the trap of believing that there are simply so many imperatives they can't even think about where to start. Psychologists call this 'agglomeration' (see also Chapter 6). Literally meaning 'a jumbled mess', in tough times some people find that they can't see a way forward, let alone know how to tackle the inherent complexities of a situation. They end up feeling dispirited and helpless.

If you experience this, the only way to make progress is to break the problem down. Like much good advice, this is conceptually simple but often very difficult to do in practice – you might require help from a mentor, coach, friend or trusted confidant. Once you have identified the component parts of any problem, it is then a question of prioritizing and taking first things first. Breaking the cycle of inaction can, in itself, spur you on to greater things; it's often taking that first small step which makes all the difference.

3 I only get one shot at this

Another excuse for inaction is the belief that you only have one chance to get it right. In some situations, this is quite correct. But more often it's not, especially in circumstances where even the old hands can't predict the right way to go – a politically-charged dilemma for example, where there are many different views, agendas and proposed resolutions. It then becomes a question of trial and error, always being alert to what the worst-case scenario might be, and carefully thinking through any unintended consequences.

4 There's a right answer to everything

A linked belief is that there is a right answer to everything, and that by thorough analysis you will surely arrive at that answer. You will then know which way to turn. Unfortunately, life rarely works out like this; it is far more complex and chaotic. There is a real risk, therefore, that the search for this 'perfect answer' becomes a displacement activity; that analysis becomes a substitute for, rather than a prelude to, action.

5 I am on my own

In tough times, many people feel as though they are the only ones who are suffering, that they have no one to talk to, and that they have to weather the storm alone. This leads to feelings of isolation and desperation, and means that those affected miss the opportunity to get ideas and support from elsewhere. If you confide in another person, not only will you get things off your chest but you might also get the chance to demonstrate empathy with a fellow sufferer. On the whole, talking things through is a sign of strength not weakness, although, as mentioned back in Chapter 9, you do need to choose your confidant well.

6 This isn't fair

There is considerable evidence in the medical world which suggests that perpetrators heal more quickly than victims – after road accidents, for example. This carries through into the world of psychology; if you believe that you have in some way contributed to the problem, you are more likely to feel accountable for resolving it. The corollary of this is that if you feel you are not to blame, that the problem or situation is not of your doing and is therefore unfair, you may dwell on this fact, rather than focusing on what can be done to make things better. While this response is totally understandable, it is a complete waste of valuable time and energy.

We talked in Chapter 5 about the attitudes, emotions, behaviours and outcomes model. This is reproduced opposite, but this time with the first of the 'drag anchors' identified on page 166 fuelling the cycle, illustrating what happens when you think in this way.

Attitudes, emotions, behaviours and outcomes model, example

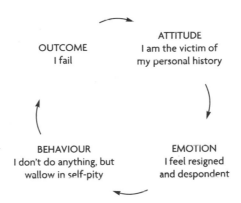

OUTCOME
I fail

ATTITUDE
I am the victim of
my personal history

BEHAVIOUR
I don't do anything, but
wallow in self-pity

EMOTION
I feel resigned
and despondent

In order to break out of this cycle – turning a vicious circle into a virtuous one – many people find that it helps to reframe their thinking. Here are the drag anchor examples given earlier – in their original, unconstructive (negative) form – and then once reframed.

Unconstructive thought	Reframed thought
✗ I am the victim of my personal history	✓ I can take control of my own destiny – and will
✗ There's so much to do, it's not even worth trying	✓ Let me break the problem down and work out which parts can be tackled now
✗ I only get one shot at this	✓ I'll do my best to get it right, but if it doesn't work out, I can have another go
✗ There's a right answer to everything	✓ Let's just give it our best shot and do what we can to set things up to succeed
✗ I am on my own	✓ I'm absolutely not on my own; there are many people out there willing to help
✗ This isn't fair	✓ There's no point complaining, I need to get on and put things right

4 Become more optimistic

'Resilience is the ability to reframe things, most notably moving from feeling disappointment to seeing opportunities.'

Optimism is one of the most important characteristics of resilient people; it's really important to look on the bright side, to have confidence in your own ability to sort issues out, to salvage what can be salvaged from problematic situations.

Even if you lean towards the 'glass half empty' mindset, it is possible to learn to be optimistic. The reframing technique mentioned in the previous section is very useful on this front too. If you are thinking, 'This is impossible – I can't cope', turning this around into something like, 'I've handled situations like this before and they've always turned out well, so let me just stop and think what are the most important things to do now' is obviously a more optimistic frame of mind, which will have a positive impact on your emotions, and encourage constructive behaviours. Getting into the discipline of reframing will help enormously.

We talked in Chapter 4 about Martin Seligman's concept of 'learned optimism'. Seligman advocates a five-stage 'ABCDE' process; this is outlined below.

A is for Adversity
This is all about acknowledging the adverse situation that triggered feelings of helplessness in you.

B is for Beliefs
An adverse situation will generate a set of beliefs. This stage of the process involves exploring your beliefs – both positive and negative.

C is for Consequences

Once you have examined the beliefs generated by the adverse situation, it is then important to analyze what the consequences of these beliefs might be. Returning to the previous example, if your belief is, 'I can't cope with this; it's just too difficult', it is likely that the result will indeed be a failure to cope. At this stage it is also important to consider what the worst-case scenario might be; is it *really* so bad?

D is for Disputation

This involves challenging any negative beliefs by finding evidence to dispute them, and then generating alternatives to these beliefs.

E is for Energization

This is all about noticing what happens to your energy levels as you dispel and deal with any negative beliefs.

Seligman's process is conceptually simple, although it can take a real act of will and considerable discipline to make it a reality. If you tend towards pessimism, you first need to recognize this; you then need to want to change it. And once the desire is there, you actually have to effect the change. Perhaps the best way of shifting your approach is to keep a log – a notebook with the pages divided into sections headed 'A', 'B', 'C', 'D' and 'E'. When something bad happens, you work through the five stages of this A, B, C, D, E process in a disciplined manner. For some people, writing things down is not their preferred approach; they'd rather think issues through in their heads. This is fair enough, but many people who fall into this camp find that doing something that goes against the grain adds to the impact of the exercise, making it more rigorous and robust. So, do try to get your thoughts down on paper or onto your laptop.

As well as making you more optimistic, this discipline also gets you into a problem-solving frame of mind and helps start the planning process – what do you actually need to *do* in order to address the problem? In this way, it enables you to be a pragmatic optimist, rather than someone with their head stuck obliviously in the sand.

5 Manage your stress

> 'Resilience is about keeping going in stressful situations, not allowing yourself to be got down, and motivating other people to do the same.'

> 'Resilience gives you the ability to handle whatever comes your way while retaining confidence, balance and control. You may be feeling stressed (or even, perhaps, out of control), but you know you can handle it.'

As mentioned in Chapter 6, some personality types are more prone to stress than others. Type B people have been described as having a 'healthy' stress response, while Type A and Type C people sit at two opposite ends of a continuum – the former having an 'arousal' stress response and the latter an 'immune-suppressing' stress response. It is vital that you understand which category most closely reflects your personality type – and the implications of this. For example, if you are Type A, it's worth recognizing that some of your characteristics will be useful in helping you to succeed. You need, therefore, to capitalize on the positive aspects of your personality, and eliminate any stress-inducing elements, such as:

- Displaying hostility towards others
- Being generally critical of others
- Being too much of a perfectionist
- Being unable to listen properly to others

- Having a tendency to hide your feelings
- Having difficulty relaxing

By contrast, if you are Type C, you need to get into the habit of sharing more, difficult though this might be for you. You also need to make sure that you have some kind of safety valve in place – an outlet for your emotions. Once you have considered the implications of your personality, the next step is to identify your stressors. These vary enormously from individual to individual, so you need to be very clear about what specifically causes *you* stress. Is it having too much to do, or maybe too little? If you cannot eliminate these stressors, you need to categorize them in terms of which can be managed or reduced.

Is it possible for you to reframe your thinking about any of your stressors, perhaps getting things more into perspective, or just reacting in a different way? Although reframing will help reduce the number of situations in which *eustress* tips over into *distress*, it won't get rid of them altogether. You therefore need to have strategies for dealing with stress when it risks becoming debilitating for you.

As mentioned in Chapter 6, these strategies fall into two distinct categories – distraction and resolution. Distraction techniques include taking exercise, writing things down or talking through issues with other people. Resolution is focused more on solving the problem that's causing the stress. These two strategies are not mutually exclusive – one may precede the other – but they are both immensely useful. What's more, there's no doubt that the ability to change your state – for example, from panicked, angry and frustrated to calm, rational and constructive – really helps. Deep breathing or even meditation can do this for you. There are also techniques, advocated by practitioners of Neuro-Linguistic Programming (NLP), which help you to achieve this 'state change' instantaneously. One such technique involves summoning up personal resources; the learning process for this is described below.

1   Identify a current difficult issue for you
2   Think about the personal resources you would need in that situation in order to handle it in the best possible way. Try to list three personal resources. Examples might include a sense of perspective, confidence, enjoyment, feeling articulate, and so on
3   For each of these personal resources, identify a situation in your past – either private or professional – in which you have possessed this personal resource in abundance (identify a separate situation for each of the three personal resources)
4   Return to the first experience you identified (in which you possessed the first personal resource). See what you saw, hear what you heard, feel what you felt – really *be* there. Dwell in the moment for up to a minute
5   'Break state' (walk around the room/shake yourself)
6   Return to the second experience you identified
7   Break state
8   Return to the third experience you identified
9   Break state
10 Now go back to the first situation once again. Summon up the personal resource and hold on to it while you return to the second situation. Hold on to the first two personal resources while you return to the third situation and summon up the third (and final) personal resource. Hold on to that state for a while – really experience it
11 Once you have mastered this, anchor the feeling (ie while in the 'resourceful state', make a physical gesture that your brain will link with that state, for example, pressing your thumb and index finger together or rubbing your ear)

Once you have mastered this technique, you will be able to use the anchor to transform your state instantaneously, as the following case study describes.

Summoning up personal resources

J was a reasonably senior lawyer, though not yet a partner. She was technically excellent, and clients valued her input – once they got to know her. But she didn't make a good first impression and tended to be tense and anxious in meetings. This caused her a great deal of negative stress and she knew that she needed to modify her behaviour or she'd never make partner. However, this realization made things worse; she felt as though the pressure was really on, and her anxiety levels increased yet further.

J tried on many occasions to relax and come across with greater confidence, but without success, and so the firm she worked for recommended an executive coach. The coach introduced her to the technique of 'summoning up personal resources' and helped her to master it.

It was easy to pinpoint the difficult situation that needed to be addressed – any meeting with senior, unfamiliar clients, made worse by the presence of one or two of her partner colleagues.

After some consideration, J established that, in order to perform well in these situations, she would have to possess the following three personal resources:

1 Confidence
2 Credibility
3 The ability to think on her feet

She then needed to identify situations in her past when she'd possessed these personal resources in abundance. As far as 'confidence' was concerned, although she was reasonably confident at work, this was nothing compared with the way she had felt at a friend's wedding a few months earlier when she'd made a very successful speech. So she chose that experience for the exercise.

The second personal resource was 'credibility', and this was straightforward for J; she had designed and run a training session for newly-qualified lawyers earlier that year. Because she had researched and prepared so carefully, she came across with immense credibility.

As for the third resource – 'the ability to think on her feet' – this was much more difficult. Reflective by nature, J was not used to answering questions immediately, preferring to go away, think about things, and then come back with a reply. However, after racking her brains, it occurred to her that one or two of the committees she was on required her to demonstrate this very ability. So she chose the practice group strategy committee, since this was particularly challenging.

During the exercise, she closed her eyes and first 'returned' to her friend's wedding. She conjured up the guests, the room – everything she'd seen at the time. She heard her own voice making the speech – and the appreciative laughter. And, importantly, she re-experienced her feelings. As she did so, it became very clear to J what the personal resource of 'confidence' felt like.

Then she 'broke state', walking around the room and shaking out her arms.

She repeated this, both for the training session and the practice group strategy committee, on each occasion paying particular attention to what the personal resource felt like.

So far so good, but the next part was the most difficult. This involved once again returning to each situation, in turn, but on this occasion she needed to 'hold on' to the personal resources, combining 'credibility' with 'confidence', and then – while experiencing both these resources – adding 'the ability to think on her feet' to the mix.

It took a number of attempts, but on her third go, J said that she felt a wave of energy pass through her body, and she experienced a sensation of 'opening up'. To 'anchor' this feeling, she pressed hard on her knee. Her brain then made the connection between this gesture and the resourceful state, which meant that, in a difficult meeting, J only needed to press her knee to feel the confidence, credibility and ability to think on her feet come flooding back to her.

J used the technique very successfully for years - and not just in client meetings, but in any situation where she felt the need to come across at her most resourceful best. J said that the technique helped her to regain control in stressful situations and to convey the right impression, no matter how difficult things became. Needless to say, she made partner!

Checklist

✓ Look ahead. What potentially stress-inducing events are on the horizon? What can you do to reduce their negative impact on you, or even eliminate them altogether?

✓ When eustress tips over into distress, analyze *exactly* what's causing you the problem

✓ Establish whether a distraction strategy or a resolution strategy would work best for you – or, indeed, whether you need both!

✓ Breathe deeply

✓ Regain perspective

✓ Change your state

✓ Act!

6 Improve your decision-making

Resilience allows (and requires) you to take action. Taking action involves making, not avoiding, decisions. Resilient people do not avoid decisions; they are proactive and believe firmly in a flexible approach. They trust their judgement, but are not afraid to change their minds. Perhaps this is one reason why they find decision-making easy – experience tells them that decisions are rarely irrevocable. To make progress in this, you need to take some action, so make the best decision that you can and get on with it!

As discussed in Chapter 7, there is a two-stage analysis process which helps you determine your own decision-making style. The first involves establishing the extent to which you are avoidant. The second covers the approach you adopt when you do take a decision (no matter when or how rare that is).

If you are avoidant by nature, you probably need to rein in this tendency; it is damaging to your RQ. It is difficult to say exactly what you need to do to address this other than to take a risk, make a judgement, but address it you must, because procrastination and prevarication are the enemies of resilience. Building your experience, working hard to trust your own judgement and seeking rapid reassurance from others might also help boost confidence in your decision-making.

Tips

✓ Evaluate the real risk – what's the worst-case scenario?

✓ Talk to others or do some homework – anything to help speed up your decision-making process

✓ Be honest – what's the point of putting off this decision?

✓ Take some action now – what could you do as a small first step?

✓ Build confidence in your ability to take decisions – how many times has it worked for you? How many times has it actually gone wrong?

✓ Change the way you see yourself – you *are* someone who can be decisive

Moving on to the second stage, you then need to determine your preferred decision-making approach. Are you rational and independent or intuitive and consultative? There are four possible combinations. Which are you?

It is important to play to individual strengths, so it is helpful to establish the situations in which your natural style is most appropriate. One way to help you understand this is to identify circumstances where your preferred approach might *not* be the best way. For example, if you have an urgent decision to make about which mortgage to take out, an intuitive, consultative approach might not serve you well – it takes too long and it could be overly emotional. By contrast, if you are trying to persuade a large number of people around to your way of thinking on a sensitive issue, a rational and independent approach might well produce a sensible answer, but will it secure the buy-in you need from other people?

Below are some tips and tactics to help you shift your style.

Shifting your style

Becoming more intuitive	Becoming more rational
✓ Build experience ✓ Gain a real understanding of the shortcuts you employ when taking decisions ✓ Learn to read your physical signals ✓ Establish the worst-case scenario ✓ Take a risk ✓ Learn	✓ Stand back – don't rush to judgement ✓ Gather data ✓ Talk to the relevant parties ✓ Establish decision-making criteria – what boxes does the solution really need to tick? ✓ Use a rational decision-making process ✓ 'Sense check' the answer

GENERAL TACTICS

Regardless of whether you need to become more intuitive or more rational in your decision-making – or whether it would be beneficial for you to seek the input of others or stand on your own two feet – there are a number of general tactics you can employ to ensure your decisions are robust. These are summarized below.

Tactics

✓ Constantly remind yourself what you're trying to achieve – what is your overall objective? Perhaps you are getting bogged down with an issue that is tangential, in which case, you should move on

✓ Be clear about the assumptions that have been made in viewing any decision in a particular way

✓ Always consider the decision from as many different angles as possible. How would you feel about the situation if everything had been framed positively, or negatively?

✓ Pay special attention to any evidence that contradicts your opinion. It is easy to ignore such opinion because it makes you feel better in the short term, but it may be just what you need to hear to stop you falling into the 'sunk cost' trap described in Chapter 7

✓ Solicit other people's opinions, and be receptive. While you may think your ideas are the best, so do all the people you consult (probably!), so think about the strengths of their suggestions

✓ When asking for an opinion, only tell the person objective information about your ideas. This will avoid you unduly influencing them. Similarly, before seeking advice, make sure you've had time to cultivate your own thoughts and, preferably, write them down so you can't ignore them should you come across opposing opinions

✓ Play 'devil's advocate' with yourself and others. What's the worst that could happen? How would your enemies rubbish your idea?

✓ Consider both intended and unintended consequences of the various options – what *could* happen if you settled on a particular course of action? What's the worst-case scenario?

7 Ask for help

Resilient people know when to reach out and ask others for help. They also have a clear idea of who the best person would be to turn to in any particular situation. Do you have this strength of network? Do you have clarity about what each person in your network can offer you? If not, it might make sense for you to map it out.

Take a large sheet of paper and draw a circle in the middle. This is you. You are now going to draw your network, with the other people you know depicted within circles too. You might want to divide your page/contacts into 'professional' and 'personal', or it might be clearer to do the exercise separately for each domain.

So, who are the people you know? How strong is each relationship? To illustrate this, you could place people with whom you have a close relationship literally closer to you on the page. Those with whom you don't have much of a relationship at all could be indicated by a dotted line. Similarly, you could draw a bigger circle for people with greater importance in your life. Add links between members of your network. Build a robust picture. Once you have done this, consider what it is you want from these individuals – and what you can offer them in return – and add this to the map. Then review and reflect. What actions do you need to take to make sure that you have all the support you need from your network?

Network map model, example

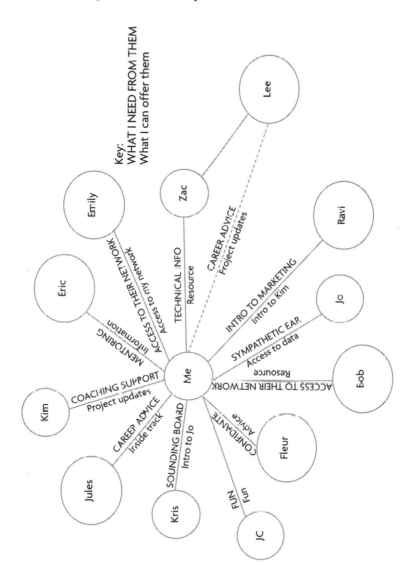

Key:
WHAT I NEED FROM THEM
What I can offer them

Lee

Zac

CAREER ADVICE
Project updates

Emily

Eric

ACCESS TO THEIR NETWORK
Access to my network

MENTORING
Information

TECHNICAL INFO
Resource

Ravi

INTRO TO MARKETING
Intro to Kim

Jo

SYMPATHETIC EAR
Access to data

Me

COACHING SUPPORT
Project updates

ACCESS TO THEIR NETWORK
Resource

Bob

Kim

CAREER ADVICE
Inside track

SOUNDING BOARD
Intro to Jo

CONFIDANTE
Advice

Fleur

Jules

FUN
Fun

Kris

JC

Once you have conducted your analysis, you need to think about how you can succeed in implementing your plan – how you can build strong relationships with those you have identified as being important. Returning to Stephen Covey's emotional bank account for a moment, remember that networking is a two-way process – there is give as well as take, deposits as well as withdrawals.

8 Deal with conflict
The Thomas Kilmann approach to conflict resolution was outlined in Chapter 10.

Clearly, if you are going to increase your resilience, it is essential to acknowledge and face up to differences of opinion. You then need to know which style is appropriate in which circumstance, and to have the flexibility to adopt whichever is the most relevant. A word of caution, however; as conflicts vary so much, both in their nature and in the personalities of those involved, it is difficult to legislate for all eventualities. Use the following as a framework to help you assess which style to use when, but remember to think through your approach quite carefully in each individual situation, always bearing in mind the *specific outcome* you want to achieve.

Competing
Competing is highly assertive and not very cooperative – the style to use when you're sure your way is the right way. It doesn't always have to be directive, however; it can be immensely charismatic – a persuasive 'sell'. Here are some tips to help you compete effectively.

Tips

✓ Be assertive, not aggressive (ie confident in expressing your needs, wants and opinions in a respectful, not hostile manner)

✓ Avoid emotive language

✓ Be clear about what you want to achieve

✓ Make it easy for the other person to say 'yes' to you by getting inside their head and understanding how what you want might also be good for them

✓ Point out benefits

✓ Make it seem as though your proposed solution was their idea

✓ Be gracious in victory

Accommodating

An accommodating style is the opposite of competing; it is highly cooperative and not very assertive. It is the approach you would adopt when you are happy for the other person to have their way.

Tips

✓ Calmly point out that this would not be your preferred solution, but, in the interests of the relationship, you'd be happy to...

✓ Set the proposed resolution in the longer-term context (ie get some credit in the emotional bank account)

✓ Make sure that the other person doesn't think that this sets a precedent – establish appropriate conditions

✓ Don't resent accommodating – you need to come to terms with (and feel good about) going along with the other person's wishes

Avoiding

Avoiding should only really be used when the matter is totally trivial (choose your battles), when you know that no resolution is possible, or when it makes far more sense for someone else to sort out the issue.

Tips

✓ Avoid for the right reasons (not just because you can't face confronting the issue)

✓ Try to feel OK about avoiding; come to terms with it

✓ Put the matter out of your head

Compromising

Compromising is more of a half-way house; both parties get some (but not all) of what they want. A compromise solution is really only appropriate for issues which are not very significant, or when a quick answer is required.

Tips

✓ Use your negotiation skills (compromising is a very similar process), ie try to give way on points which don't matter to you, but don't compromise on points that do

✓ Manage expectations – all parties need to understand that they probably won't be totally satisfied and (ideally) buy in to this fact

✓ Accept that things won't be perfect

✓ Try to get the best result you can

Collaborating

Collaborating is appropriate for the resolution of issues which are important. This approach can take some time, but is worth it in the long run since it enables both parties to get to a result they feel happy with. Collaboration may not be appropriate for trivial matters. Below are some tips that will help you collaborate effectively.

Tips

✓ Prepare beforehand, but don't allow this to get in the way of open-mindedness

✓ Position the matter very carefully – be positive, opportunity-focused and future-orientated

✓ Explain the process (as formally or informally as you like), and make sure that the other person is happy with it

✓ Express your genuine desire to resolve the issue

✓ Elicit feedback and listen actively to it; ask 'open' questions (ones that do not demand a simple 'yes' or 'no' response). Be genuinely interested in what the other person has to say (this might require reframing on your part)

✓ Avoid seeming defensive or aggressive; maintain an interested stance throughout

✓ Give your feedback/perspective

✓ Summarize both positions, including areas of agreement and disagreement. Get things into perspective

✓ Ask how you (plural) can take things forward

✓ Listen to the other person's suggestions – build on them, add your own, and cross-check that suggested solutions actually resolve the issue; generate options

✓ Collectively agree the way forward

Since this is such a powerful and important method of resolving conflict – but one that many people struggle to adopt – a step-by-step process is outlined opposite.

Following this process will help ensure that you are genuinely collaborating, that it's not just another of the styles masquerading as being collaborative!

Collaborative conflict resolution model

Define your desired outcome
- Think the issue through in advance
- Be clear and honest about the best outcome for you
- Try to anticipate what the other party will want

Position the meeting
- Introduce the objective and process
- State your desire to resolve the issue
- Gain the other party's agreement to the process

Understand their perspective
- Ask for their perspective on the matter
- Listen actively
- Ask questions to ensure you clearly understand

Share your perspective
- Share your perspective with them
- Encourage them to listen actively to you
- Where appropriate, make links to what they have said

Summarize
- Summarize the areas which need to be resolved
- Summarize the two positions
- Emphasize the areas in which there is agreement

Discuss possibilities
- Agree what you both ideally want going forward
- Generate suggestions
- Discuss and evaluate the possibilities

Agree a way forward
- Agree the best way forward
- Agree next steps
- Act!

9 Learn

Many resilient individuals ask themselves, 'What have I learnt today?' They passionately believe in lifelong learning – for them, to stand still would mean complete stagnation, death almost.

> 'I never want to be in the position of saying, "I could have done that if I'd tried". I must learn from my experiences and achieve as much as I can, whatever I'm doing.'

Thinking about what happens to you each day, and what lessons can be drawn from your experiences, strengthens your 'learning muscle' and helps you build resilience. We strongly recommend that you get into this habit. Before doing this, however, you need to understand *how* you learn.

Back in the 1970s, Peter Honey and Alan Mumford developed a learning styles system while working on a project for the Chloride corporation. Honey and Mumford coined the terms 'activist', 'reflector', 'theorist' and 'pragmatist' to describe the different ways in which people learn. *Activists* learn through doing, while *reflectors* absorb information by reading, observing or listening to others. *Theorists* are concerned with intellectual rigour and concepts, while *pragmatists* focus on practical considerations, 'How does this work?' 'How can it be implemented?' 'What can I do?'

Consider these four styles of learning. Which one are you? How do you best learn? Knowing the answer to these questions will help you to take the most from the experiences life throws at you.

Similarly, you might want to consider whether you are predominantly visual, auditory or kinesthetic.

A visual person literally sees things, and so relates more to pictures than to words, which are the preference for the auditory person. The kinesthetic likes to 'touch and feel', so requires lessons to be brought to life. Again, it is crucial to know your own preference. How does your brain work? If you are visual, you are unlikely to absorb much from large, wordy tomes. Instead, you prefer diagrams and pictures, whether reviewing them or creating them. The ideal learning experience for you might involve mapping out what has gone wrong and then developing models and processes which will help to avoid the problem occurring again. If, by contrast, you are predominantly auditory, you have the ability to absorb a lot of words – spoken or written – and so will learn from oral briefings, books or other materials. And, as already mentioned, the kinesthetic needs to be able to relate to experiences. If you are kinesthetic, lots of case studies, anecdotes and experiential learning will work best for you.

Getting into the habit of learning, doing it daily to flex your learning muscle, and ensuring that your learning experiences are the most effective for your personality type, will all help you continue to develop personally throughout your life. And lifelong learning not only helps you develop, it also fuels enhanced resilience.

Tips

✓ Invest the time for learning – schedule it and stick to it

✓ Ensure that you are in a receptive frame of mind to learn

✓ Examine your motivation – what's in it for you to change things going forward? How *could* you motivate yourself to do things differently next time?

✓ Conduct the post-mortem, with others or on your own

✓ Be mindful – fixated with failure as a means of learning from your mistakes

✓ Role model others – identify people who do it well and learn from them

✓ Research, research, research!

10 Be yourself

One of the main reasons why people don't change is that the 'new, improved version' is not actually in keeping with the way they have come to view themselves – it's just not them. Whether this is acknowledged by the individual or is subconscious, if what they are (in theory) supposed to be moving towards is misaligned with their identity or values, it just won't happen. So, if you want to enhance your resilience, you need also to remain true to yourself – you must be *authentic* – which requires a strong sense of your identity and values.

Surprising though this might seem, many people are not totally clear about this, which means they sometimes just don't understand why they don't approve of a particular idea or fail to implement a plan when they're normally so action-orientated.

Using the logical levels model described in Chapter 3 (page 43), map out who you are. An example is given opposite.

Of course, this is just an illustration. When you do this exercise for real, you are likely to have more points at each level. But once you've captured these, be discerning – which are the really important ones? Highlight these, then use this information to help you determine appropriate courses of action (for example, is this in line with my values?), and to ensure that you are, indeed, being yourself.

Logical levels model, example

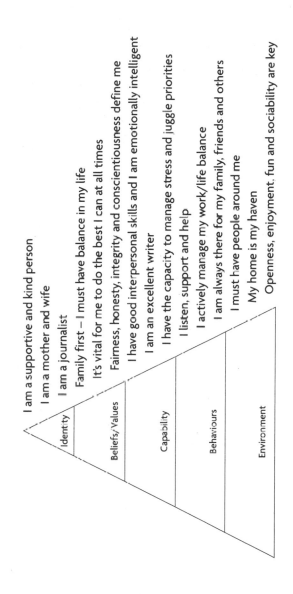

RESILIENCE, REFORM AND REVOLUTION

When it comes to changing yourself, resilience can be a double-edged sword. On the one hand, some of its elements – for example, optimism, being relatively immune to the effects of stress, and being eager to take control for achieving outcomes – would seem to be useful resources to bring to the personal transformation party. On the other hand, the ability to keep going when times are tough, or to reframe your feelings when you find yourself in an uncomfortable position, could work the other way, giving a very resilient person the ability to stick with an unpromising position rather than seeking to change things.

The key here, then, is flexibility. Resilient people are flexible in their approach to people, problems and environment. They know when to cut their losses, and when to go the extra mile. They know how to reframe experiences and get the most out of any situation. They know how to learn. Resilient people are nature's reformers, rather than revolutionaries. Are you ready to join the ranks of the resilient?

Conclusion

We first started thinking about this book during a period of considerable economic turbulence and uncertainty – the 2008 'credit crunch'. The crunch had devastating consequences; stocks went through the floor, unemployment through the roof. While, as we write today, key economic indicators such as house prices, markets and personal wealth have all bounced back to something like pre-crunch levels, the recovery is still fragile. This, then, has been a remarkable time in which to be studying resilience. As a psychological quality, or an approach to life, resilience can rarely have been more at a premium.

But we have not found resilience to be in short supply. Indeed, we have been amazed by people's powers of resilience in tough times – how they have managed to deal with the curve ball.

In our work as coaches, we supported many people on the front line of the credit crunch; our understanding of the origins and nature of resilience has been profoundly influenced by the way in which these individuals responded to the significant challenges they faced.

We have also learnt a great deal from our encounters with the R-team. While the members of the R-team are exceptional individuals in many respects, we are convinced that they actually represent an extreme manifestation of a quality we all possess. Resilience is innate; it just needs to be nurtured, boosted and unleashed when required – which may well mean now.

Go on, hit that curve ball out of the park!

Appendix

EVIDENCE FROM THE NICHOLSON MCBRIDE RESILIENCE QUESTIONNAIRE (NMRQ)

We have already reported many of the early findings of the NMRQ in the main sections of the book. In this appendix, we present evidence relating to the impact of generic factors such as gender, stage of life and work experience – including the significance of experiencing redundancy – on the development of resilience.

Gender

Overall, men rated themselves as significantly more resilient than women. For the first cohort (334 respondents), the average RQ score for men was 68.2% compared with 65.6% for women.

In terms of individual items, men are more likely to agree with the following statements:

- I am calm in a crisis
- I enjoy ambiguity
- I try not to take things too seriously

- People describe me as being laid back
- I influence what I can rather than worrying about what I can't
- I've generally found that things turn out in an advantageous way for me
- I am more resilient than most people

Women are more likely than men to agree with the following statements:

- I can empathize with others very well
- I prefer stability to ambiguity
- I always try to muddle through
- I tend to avoid conflict wherever possible
- I can be a bit insecure at times
- People say I give myself a hard time
- I tend to get stressed quite easily
- I would describe myself as an anxious person
- I tend to take criticism personally
- I am more intuitive than rational in my decision-making
- I am prone to 'analysis paralysis'
- I would like to be more resilient

Stage of life and work experience

Analysis of the early data from the NMRQ also reveals that, over a 'typical' 40-year career, both men and women tend to become more resilient. Analysis of individual NMRQ items explains how this happens. Consider first what our respondents tell us about the feelings and behaviours that promote resilience. On some items, scores rise steadily over the working decades. Such items include:

- People tell me they respect me
- I never sweep things under the carpet
- I enjoy ambiguity

Similarly, some characteristics which are known to undermine resilience clearly decline over the years. For example:

- I can't always see the wood for the trees
- I am prone to 'analysis paralysis'
- I am prone to procrastination
- I compare myself regularly to others
- I quite envy other people

Other developmental trends are less regular, but still significant. For example, older respondents are less likely to talk about 'muddling through' or worrying about what other people think of them. They are more comfortable with ambiguity, less concerned with avoiding conflict, and less troubled about admitting that they have changed their mind. They are also more likely to be described as 'laid back', and are more willing to concede that it is possible to be too resilient! The latter may be a significant finding in light of our warning at the end of Chapter 11 that certain aspects of resilience can reduce flexibility, thereby creating the possibility that extreme resilience becomes a handicap rather than an advantage. Confidence in being able to create success from disaster grows dramatically during the first decade at work, and remains at a consistently high level thereafter.

Where redundancy is concerned, just over a quarter of those who have completed the NMRQ to date have first-hand experience of this. Compared with those without this experience, these people are – unsurprisingly – less likely to report that they feel 'secure in their position'. They distinguish themselves in three other respects. First, they are significantly less likely to report that when things go wrong for them it's usually because they have acted without thinking through the consequences of their actions. Secondly, they are more likely to agree with the statement, 'people tell me that they respect me'. Finally, they are significantly more likely to respond positively to the statement, 'I tend to bounce back from knocks'. These results may explain why respondents who have experienced redundancy tend to have a higher overall RQ than those who have not, although the difference between the two groups is not significant. Similarly, although our data reveal a link between level of income and Resilience Quotient – the more you earn, the more resilient you rate yourself – this difference too falls just short of statistical significance.

THE CONTRIBUTION OF INDIVIDUAL NMRQ ITEMS TO THE FIVE KEY ELEMENTS OF RESILIENCE

Here are the NMRQ items which statistically have been found to contribute most to a person's score on each of the five key elements of resilience (see page 15), and the way in which they do so, ie positively (+) or negatively (-).

Optimism
- I've generally found that things turn out in an advantageous way for me (+)
- I am good at seeing the silver lining (+)
- In a difficult situation, my thoughts immediately turn to what can be done to put things right (+)
- I am calm in a crisis (+)
- I tend to bounce back from knocks (+)
- I trust my intuition (+)

Freedom from stress and anxiety
- I manage my stress levels well (+)
- I can be a bit insecure at times (-)
- I tend to take criticism personally (-)

- I quite envy other people (-)
- I could do more to keep things in perspective (-)
- I am poor at knowing when to move on (-)

Individual accountability

- I feel confident and secure in my position (+)
- I often worry what people think about me (-)
- I tend to avoid conflict wherever possible (-)
- I often decide that an issue is too difficult to tackle (-)
- I am prone to 'analysis paralysis' (-)
- I can't always see the wood for the trees (-)

Openness and flexibility

- I am flexible (+)
- I influence what I can rather than worrying about what I can't (+)
- I can empathize with others very well (+)
- People tell me they respect me (+)
- I prefer stability to ambiguity (-)
- I find myself making the same mistakes again and again (-)

Problem orientation

- I can often create success from disaster (+)
- I am good at finding solutions to new problems (+)
- I am good at anticipating problems (+)
- I try to control events rather than being a victim of my circumstances (+)
- I am well known for making sound judgements (+)
- I know when to cut my losses (+)

Bibliography and further reading

Amato, JA and RL McMasters, *Golf Beats Us All (And So We Love It)* (Johnson: CO, 1997)

Bandura, A, 'Self-efficacy: toward a unifying theory of behavioral change', *Psychological Review*, 84, 191–215, 1977

Barlow, DH, Lehrer, PM, Woolfolk, RL and WE Sime, *Principles and Practice of Stress Management* (Guilford, 3rd edition: New York, 2008)

Carnegie, D, *How to Win Friends and Influence People* (Pocket: New York, 1988)

Clarke, J and L Nichols, *Wired Working: Thriving in a connected world* (Spiro: London, 2002)

Clarke, J, *Office Politics: A survival guide* (The Industrial Society: London, 1999)

Cohen-Charash, Y and Jennifer S Mueller, 'Does perceived unfairness exacerbate or mitigate interpersonal counterproductive work behaviors related to envy?', *Journal of Applied Psychology*, 92(3), 666–680, 2007

Conner, DR, *Managing at the Speed of Change: How resilient managers succeed and prosper where others fail* (Villard: New York, 1992)

Cooper, CL and P Dewe, *Stress: A brief history* (Blackwell: Oxford, 2004)

Coutu, DL, 'How resilience works', *Harvard Business Review*, 80(5), 2002

Covey, SR, *The 7 Habits of Highly Effective People* (Simon & Schuster: New York, 1989)

Crocker, J and CT Wolfe, 'Contingencies of self-worth', *Psychological Review*, 108(3), 593– 623, 2001

Dilts, R, *Applications of Neuro-Linguistic Programming* (Meta: CA, 1983)

Dittmann, M, 'After the wave', *Monitor on Psychology*, 36(3), 36, 2005

Dotlich, DL and PC Cairo, *Why CEOs Fail: The 11 behaviors that can derail your climb to the top – and how to manage them* (Jossey-Bass: San Francisco, 2003)

Drucker, P, *Peter Drucker on the Profession of Management* (Harvard Business School Press: Cambridge, MA, 1998)

D'Souza, S, *Brilliant Networking: What the best networkers know, say and do* (Prentice Hall: New Jersey, 2007)

Fernando, GA, 'Interventions for survivors of the tsunami disaster: report from Sri Lanka', *Journal of Traumatic Stress*, 18(3), 267–8, 2005

Finkelstein, S, Whitehead, J and A Campbell, *Think Again: Why good leaders make bad decisions and how to stop it from happening to you* (Harvard Business School Press: Cambridge, MA, 2009)

Fisher, R, Ury, W and B Patton, *Getting to Yes: Negotiating an agreement without giving in* (Penguin: New York, 1991)

Flaherty, J, *Coaching: Evoking excellence in others* (Butterworth-Heinemann, 2nd edition: Burlington, MA, 2005)

Friedman, M and RH Rosenman, *Type A Behavior and your Heart* (Knopf: New York, 1974)

Giltay, EJ, Geleijnse, JM, Zitman, FG, Hoekstra, T and EG Schouten, 'Dispositional optimism and all-cause and cardiovascular mortality in a prospective cohort of elderly Dutch men and women', *Archives of General Psychiatry*, 61, 1126–1135, 2004

Gladwell, M, *Blink: The power of thinking without thinking* (Penguin: London, 2006)

Gladwell, M, *Outliers: The story of success* (Little Brown: New York, 2008)

Goldstein, N, Martin, S and R Cialdini, *Yes! 50 secrets from the science of persuasion* (Profile: London, 2007)

Goleman, D, *Emotional Intelligence: Why it can matter more than IQ* (Bantam: New York, 1995)

Hanton, S, Evans, L and R Neil, 'Hardiness and the competitive trait anxiety response', *Anxiety, Stress and Coping: An international journal*, 16(2), 167–184, 2003

Hart, LB, *The Manager's Pocket Guide to Dealing with Conflict* (HRD Press: Amherst, MA, 1999)

Honey, P and A Mumford, *The Manual of Learning Styles* (Peter Honey: Maidenhead, 1982)

Howell, JM and BJ Avolio, 'Transformational leadership, transactional leadership, locus of control, and support for innovation: key predictors of consolidated-business-unit performance', *Journal of Applied Psychology*, 78(6), 891–902, 1993

Landsberg, M, *The Tao of Coaching: Boost your effectiveness at work by inspiring and developing those around you* (Profile: London, 2002)

Lin, YC and Priya Raghubir, 'Gender differences in unrealistic optimism about marriage and divorce: are men more optimistic and women more realistic?', *Asia Pacific Advances in Consumer Research*, 6, 345–346, 2005

McCall, MW, Lombardo, MM and AM Morrison, *Lessons of Experience: How successful executives develop on the job* (Free Press: New York, 1988)

Moskovitz, S, *Love Despite Hate: Child survivors of the holocaust* (Schocken: New York, 1988)

Nicholson, J, *How Do You Manage? How to make the most of yourself and your people* (BBC: London, 1992)

Nicholson, J, *Men and Women: How different are they?* (OUP, 2nd edition: Oxford, 1993)

Nicholson, J, *Seven Ages: The truth about life crises – does your age really matter?* (Fontana: Glasgow, 1980)

O'Connor, J, *NLP Workbook: A practical guide to achieving the results you want* (Thorsons: London, 2001)

Scott, SG and RA Bruce, 'Decision-making style: the development and assessment of a new measure', *Educational and Psychological Measurement*, 55(5), 818–831, 1995

Segerstrom, SC, *The Glass Half Full: How optimists get what they want from life – and pessimists can too* (Constable & Robinson: London, 2009)

Seligman, MEP, *Authentic Happiness: Using the new positive psychology to realize your potential for lasting fulfilment* (WS Bookwell: Finland, 2002)

Seligman, MEP, *Learned Optimism: How to change your mind and your life* (Knopf: New York, 1990)

Selye, H, *Stress without Distress* (McClelland & Stewart: Toronto, 1974)

Temoshok, L and H Dreher, *Type C Connection: The mind–body link to cancer and your health* (Plume: New York, 1993)

Tett, G, *Fool's Gold: How unrestrained greed corrupted a dream, shattered global markets and unleashed a catastrophe* (Little, Brown: London, 2009)

Thaler, RH and CR Sunstein, *Nudge: Improving decisions about health, wealth and happiness* (Penguin: London, 2009)

The Mind Gym: Wake your mind up (Sphere: London, 2005)

Thomas, KW, 'Conflict and conflict management: reflections and update', *Journal of Organizational Behavior*, 13(3), 265–274, 1974

Tieger, PD and B Barron-Tieger, *The Art of Speedreading People: How to size people up and speak their language* (Little Brown: New York, 1998)

Tindle, HA, Chang, YF, Kuller, LH *et al*, 'Optimism, cynical hostility, and incident coronary heart disease and mortality in the women's health initiative', *Circulation*, 120(8), 656–662, 2009

Tolstoy, L, *Anna Karenina* (Penguin, revised edition, translated by Richard Pevear and Larissa Volokhonsky: London, 2003)

Wall, JA and RR Callister, 'Conflict and its management', *Journal of Management*, 21, 515–558, 1995

Weick, KE and KM Sutcliffe, *Managing the Unexpected: Resilient performance in an age of uncertainty* (Jossey-Bass, 2nd edition: San Francisco, 2007)

Welch, J, *Winning* (HarperCollins: New York, 2005)

Werner, EE, 'Vulnerability and resiliency in children at risk for delinquency: a longitudinal study from birth to adulthood'. In Burchard, JD and SN Burchard (Eds), *Primary Prevention of Psychopathology*, 10, 16–43, 1987

Wills, AJ, Lavric, A, Croft, GS and TL Hodgson, 'Predictive learning, prediction errors, and attention: evidence from event-related potentials and eye tracking', *Journal of Cognitive Neuroscience*, 19(5), 843–854, 2007

Wilson, TD and DT Gilbert, 'Affective forecasting', *Advances in Experimental Social Psychology*, 35, 345–411, 2003

Wright, JH, Basco, MR and ME Thase, *Learning Cognitive-Behavior Therapy: An illustrated guide* (American Psychiatric Publishing: Arlington, VA, 2006)

Yerkes, RM and JD Dodson, 'The relation of strength of stimulus to rapidity of habit-formation', *Journal of Comparative Neurology and Psychology*, (18), 459–482, 1908